A Comprehensive Guide to Digital Marketing

C. P. Kumar
Reiki Healer & Author
Roorkee - 247667, India

Copyright © 2024 C. P. Kumar

All rights reserved.

No part of this book may be reproduced or transmitted in any form or by any means, electronic or mechanical, including photocopying, recording, or by any information storage and retrieval system, without permission in writing from the author.

Disclaimer

While every effort has been made to ensure the accuracy and completeness of the content in this book, the author cannot guarantee that the information contained herein is error-free, up-to-date, or suitable for every individual circumstance.

The author shall not be held liable or responsible for any errors or omissions in the content of the book, nor for any damages, or losses that may arise from any actions taken based upon the suggestions or contents presented in the book.

Readers are advised to use their own judgment and discretion in applying the information provided in this book, and to consult with qualified professionals before taking any action based on the contents of this book. The author disclaims any and all liability or responsibility for any actions taken or not taken based on the information contained in this book.

DEDICATION

To the pioneers and innovators in the field of digital marketing, whose creativity and vision have paved the way for the advancements we enjoy today.

To the digital marketing community, whose collaborative spirit and shared knowledge continue to drive the industry forward.

And to the readers, may this comprehensive guide empower you to navigate and excel in the dynamic world of digital marketing. Your dedication to mastering these skills is a testament to your passion for growth and success.

With deep appreciation,

C. P. Kumar

CONTENTS

Copyright 2
Disclaimer 3
DEDICATION 4
PREFACE 7
Chapter 1.   Essentials of Digital Marketing 10
Chapter 2.   Introduction to Strategic SEO & AI Development 17
Chapter 3.   Advanced Search Engine Optimization (SEO) Techniques 23
Chapter 4.   Maximizing Search Engine Marketing (SEM) .. 30
Chapter 5.   Harnessing the Power of SEMrush 37
Chapter 6.   Leveraging Google Analytics for Insights and Growth 43
Chapter 7.   Market Research in the Digital World 51
Chapter 8.   Lead Generation in the Digital Age 58
Chapter 9.   Content Marketing 66
Chapter 10. Blogging for Business Success 74
Chapter 11. Social Media Marketing 79
Chapter 12. Brand Design and Digital Presence 87
Chapter 13. Effective Product Marketing in the Digital Landscape 93
Chapter 14. Digital Marketing Campaigns 101
Chapter 15. Email Marketing 108
Chapter 16. Influencer Marketing 115

Chapter 17.	Affiliate Marketing	123
Chapter 18.	Conversion Rate Optimization (CRO)	128
Chapter 19.	E-commerce Strategies	135
Chapter 20.	Mobile Marketing	141
Chapter 21.	Video Marketing	148
Chapter 22.	Local SEO	155
Chapter 23.	PHP Programming for Digital Marketers	161
Chapter 24.	Fundamentals of Management Consulting in the Digital Age	168
Chapter 25.	Leadership Development for Digital Transformation	176

Other Books by the Author 183

PREFACE

In the ever-evolving landscape of business, digital marketing has emerged as a cornerstone of modern commerce. With the rise of the internet and the proliferation of digital technologies, the way businesses interact with customers has transformed dramatically. "A Comprehensive Guide to Digital Marketing" is designed to equip marketers, business owners, and digital enthusiasts with the knowledge and tools necessary to navigate this dynamic field successfully.

The primary objective of this book is to provide a thorough understanding of digital marketing principles, strategies, and practices. It addresses the essential components of digital marketing, from foundational concepts to advanced techniques, ensuring that readers gain a holistic view of the discipline. Whether you are a seasoned marketer looking to update your skills or a novice eager to enter the field, this guide offers valuable insights to help you achieve your goals.

The journey begins with an exploration of the core concepts and strategies that define digital marketing. We delve into the role of digital marketing in modern business, highlighting its significance in driving growth and fostering customer engagement. The integration of AI into digital marketing strategies is also examined, illustrating how artificial intelligence can enhance and refine marketing efforts.

As we progress, the book delves deeper into specific areas of digital marketing. Search Engine Optimization (SEO) and Search Engine Marketing (SEM) are covered extensively, offering readers advanced techniques to boost online visibility and performance. We explore the power of tools like SEMrush and Google Analytics, demonstrating how they can be leveraged to gain insights and optimize marketing strategies.

Market research, lead generation, and content marketing are crucial components of any digital strategy. This guide provides comprehensive methods for gathering and analyzing data, attracting and converting leads, and developing effective content strategies. Social media marketing, brand design, and product marketing are also explored, offering strategies tailored to various platforms and digital environments.

In addition, the book addresses the planning and execution of digital marketing campaigns, emphasizing the importance of monitoring and optimization. Email marketing, influencer and affiliate marketing, and conversion rate optimization are examined in detail, providing readers with practical techniques to enhance their marketing efforts.

E-commerce, mobile marketing, and video marketing are vital aspects of the digital marketing ecosystem. This guide covers best practices for online retail, mobile optimization, and creating engaging video content. Local SEO strategies and the basics of PHP programming are also included, offering insights into improving local search visibility and enhancing marketing efforts through programming.

The latter part of the book focuses on management consulting and leadership development in the digital age. We explore how digital transformation is shaping management practices and the skills necessary for effective leadership in this era of rapid change.

"A Comprehensive Guide to Digital Marketing" is more than just a handbook; it is a roadmap for navigating the complexities of digital marketing. By integrating traditional marketing principles with cutting-edge digital techniques, this book aims to empower readers to achieve success in the digital marketplace. We hope that this guide serves as a valuable resource, inspiring and equipping you to excel in the ever-changing world of digital marketing.

A list of my few other published works on related topics can be found at the end of this book. You may like to explore them.

C. P. Kumar

Reiki Healer, Blogger & Author
Former Scientist 'G', National Institute of Hydrology
Roorkee - 247667, India
Web: https://www.angelfire.com/nh/cpkumar/virgo.html

Chapter 1. Essentials of Digital Marketing

Introduction

Digital marketing has become a cornerstone of modern business strategy. As the world continues to embrace digitalization, businesses must adapt to the changing landscape to remain competitive. This chapter will delve into the core concepts and strategies of digital marketing, exploring its pivotal role in contemporary business operations.

Core Concepts and Strategies

At its essence, digital marketing encompasses all marketing efforts that utilize the internet or electronic devices. Businesses leverage digital channels such as search engines, social media, email, and websites to connect with current and prospective customers. Understanding these core concepts is vital for any business aiming to succeed in the digital realm.

1. Search Engine Optimization (SEO)

Search Engine Optimization (SEO) is the practice of optimizing a website to rank higher on search engine results pages (SERPs). It involves enhancing various aspects of a website, including its content, structure, and technical elements, to improve visibility on search engines like Google. Effective SEO strategies drive organic traffic to a website, making it an essential component of digital marketing. The process includes keyword research, on-page optimization, link building, and continuous performance analysis to adapt to search engine algorithm updates.

2. Content Marketing

Content marketing focuses on creating and distributing valuable, relevant, and consistent content to attract and engage a target audience. The goal is to drive profitable customer actions by providing content that educates, entertains, or inspires. This can take various forms, including blog posts, articles, videos, infographics, podcasts, and e-books. High-quality content not only improves SEO efforts but also establishes a brand as a thought leader in its industry, fostering trust and loyalty among consumers.

3. Social Media Marketing

Social media marketing involves using social platforms like Facebook, Instagram, X (Twitter), LinkedIn, and others to promote products or services. It provides businesses with a direct line of communication with their audience, enabling them to build relationships, foster community engagement, and enhance brand visibility. Effective social media strategies include creating compelling content, engaging with followers, utilizing paid advertising options, and leveraging analytics to measure performance and refine tactics.

4. Pay-Per-Click (PPC) Advertising

Pay-Per-Click (PPC) advertising is a model where advertisers pay a fee each time their ad is clicked. It's a way to buy visits to a site rather than earning them organically. Google Ads is one of the most popular PPC platforms, allowing businesses to bid on keywords and display ads in search results. PPC campaigns require careful planning, keyword research, and continuous monitoring to ensure a good return on investment (ROI).

It's an effective way to generate immediate traffic and leads while complementing long-term SEO efforts.

5. Email Marketing

Email marketing remains one of the most effective digital marketing strategies. It involves sending targeted messages to a list of subscribers to nurture relationships, promote products, or share news and updates. Successful email marketing campaigns rely on building a quality email list, segmenting the audience for personalized messages, and creating engaging content. Automation tools can help manage and optimize email campaigns, ensuring timely and relevant communication with the audience.

6. Affiliate Marketing

Affiliate marketing is a performance-based strategy where businesses reward affiliates for driving traffic or sales through their marketing efforts. Affiliates can be bloggers, influencers, or other businesses that promote products or services to their audience. This approach expands a business's reach and leverages the influence and trust affiliates have with their followers. Setting up a successful affiliate program involves selecting the right affiliates, providing them with marketing materials, and tracking their performance.

7. Influencer Marketing

Influencer marketing leverages individuals with a significant following on social media or other online platforms to promote products or services. Influencers can sway their audience's purchasing decisions due to their credibility and relationship with their followers. Collaborating with influencers involves identifying the right partners, negotiating agreements, and developing campaigns that align with both the brand and the influencer's style. It's an effective way to reach niche markets and enhance brand authenticity.

8. Analytics and Data Analysis

Data is at the heart of digital marketing. Analytics tools like Google Analytics, social media insights, and email marketing metrics provide valuable information about campaign performance and customer behavior. By analyzing this data, businesses can make informed decisions, optimize their strategies, and improve ROI. Understanding key metrics such as traffic sources, conversion rates, click-through rates, and customer demographics is crucial for measuring success and identifying areas for improvement.

The Role of Digital Marketing in Modern Business

In the modern business landscape, digital marketing plays a critical role in achieving various organizational goals. Its importance is underscored by its ability to reach a global audience, target specific demographics, and provide measurable results.

1. Enhancing Brand Awareness

Digital marketing amplifies brand visibility across multiple channels, reaching a broader audience than traditional marketing methods. Through consistent online presence and strategic content distribution, businesses can build brand awareness and recognition. Social media platforms, in particular, allow brands to engage with users in real time, fostering a sense of community and loyalty.

2. Driving Customer Engagement

One of the most significant advantages of digital marketing is the ability to interact with customers directly. Social media, blogs, and forums provide platforms for two-way communication, enabling businesses to engage with their audience, address concerns, and gather feedback. This engagement helps build stronger relationships with customers and enhances their overall experience with the brand.

3. Targeting Specific Audiences

Digital marketing allows businesses to target specific demographics with precision. Through tools like Google Ads, Facebook Ads, and email segmentation, companies can tailor their messages to resonate with different audience segments. This targeted approach ensures that marketing efforts are more relevant and effective, increasing the likelihood of conversions.

4. Measuring and Optimizing Performance

Unlike traditional marketing, digital marketing provides detailed insights into campaign performance. Businesses can track metrics such as website traffic, conversion rates, and customer engagement in real time. This data-driven approach allows for continuous optimization, ensuring that marketing strategies remain effective and efficient. By analyzing performance metrics, businesses can identify what works and what doesn't, making necessary adjustments to improve outcomes.

5. Supporting Sales and Revenue Growth

Digital marketing directly contributes to sales and revenue growth. SEO and PPC campaigns drive traffic to websites, content marketing educates and nurtures leads, and email marketing converts prospects into customers. By integrating these strategies, businesses can create a comprehensive marketing funnel that guides customers from awareness to purchase. Additionally, digital marketing offers cost-effective solutions compared to traditional advertising, providing a higher return on investment.

6. Building Customer Loyalty

Retaining customers is as crucial as acquiring new ones. Digital marketing plays a vital role in building customer loyalty through personalized communication and ongoing engagement. Email newsletters, loyalty programs, and exclusive offers help maintain relationships with existing customers, encouraging repeat business. Social media interactions also contribute to customer satisfaction and loyalty, as they provide a platform for addressing issues and celebrating positive experiences.

7. Staying Competitive

In today's digital age, businesses must embrace digital marketing to stay competitive. Consumers increasingly rely on the internet to research products, read reviews, and make purchasing decisions. Companies that fail to establish a robust online presence risk losing market share to competitors who effectively leverage digital marketing strategies. By staying up-to-date with the latest trends and technologies, businesses can adapt to changing consumer behaviors and maintain their competitive edge.

Conclusion

Digital marketing is an indispensable aspect of modern business strategy. Its core concepts and strategies - ranging from SEO and content marketing to social media and analytics - provide businesses with the tools to reach and engage their target audience effectively. The role of digital marketing in enhancing brand awareness, driving customer engagement, targeting specific audiences, and supporting sales growth cannot be overstated. As the digital landscape continues to evolve, businesses that embrace and adapt to these changes will thrive in an increasingly competitive market.

Chapter 2. Introduction to Strategic SEO & AI Development

The digital marketing landscape has evolved dramatically over the past few decades. From the early days of keyword stuffing and rudimentary analytics, we've moved towards a sophisticated blend of art and science, where data-driven strategies and creative content go hand in hand. At the heart of this evolution are Search Engine Optimization (SEO) and Artificial Intelligence (AI). Understanding the synergy between SEO and AI is crucial for any digital marketer aiming to achieve long-term success. This chapter delves into the fundamentals of SEO and AI, their integration, and how they can be leveraged to develop a robust digital marketing strategy.

Overview of SEO and AI in Digital Marketing

Search Engine Optimization (SEO) is the process of optimizing a website to rank higher in search engine results pages (SERPs). The ultimate goal of SEO is to increase organic (non-paid) traffic to a website. SEO involves various techniques, including keyword research, on-page optimization, content creation, and link building. The primary objective is to ensure that a website is accessible to search engines and improves the chances of being found by relevant search queries.

Artificial Intelligence (AI), on the other hand, refers to the simulation of human intelligence in machines. In the context of digital marketing, AI encompasses a range of technologies, including machine learning, natural language processing (NLP), and predictive analytics. AI can analyze vast amounts of data, identify patterns, and make predictions, thereby enabling marketers to make informed decisions and optimize their strategies.

The intersection of SEO and AI represents a powerful confluence of technologies. As search engines become more sophisticated, leveraging AI to enhance SEO strategies is not just advantageous but essential. AI can automate and improve various aspects of SEO, from keyword research and content creation to user experience and link building.

The Importance of Integrating AI into SEO Strategies

Integrating AI into SEO strategies offers several benefits that can significantly enhance the effectiveness and efficiency of digital marketing efforts. One of the most critical advantages is the ability to process and analyze large volumes of data. Traditional SEO methods often involve manual analysis, which can be time-consuming and prone to errors. AI, with its data processing capabilities, can quickly analyze trends, patterns, and user behavior, providing valuable insights that can inform SEO strategies.

For instance, AI-powered tools can perform advanced keyword research by analyzing search queries, user intent, and competition. These tools can identify high-potential keywords and long-tail phrases that might not be apparent through manual research. This level of insight allows marketers to target their audience more precisely and create content that meets their needs and interests.

Content creation is another area where AI integration can make a substantial impact. AI can assist in generating high-quality, SEO-friendly content by suggesting relevant topics, optimizing content structure, and even writing portions of the content. Natural Language Processing (NLP) algorithms can analyze top-performing content in a niche and provide guidelines on style, tone, and structure, ensuring that the content resonates with the target audience and ranks well in search engines.

User experience (UX) is a crucial factor in SEO, as search engines like Google increasingly prioritize websites that offer a seamless and engaging experience. AI can enhance UX by personalizing content and recommendations based on user behavior and preferences. For example, AI algorithms can analyze user interactions and suggest personalized content, products, or services, thereby increasing engagement and reducing bounce rates.

Link building, a cornerstone of SEO, also benefits from AI integration. AI can identify high-authority websites and potential link-building opportunities by analyzing backlink profiles and identifying patterns in successful link-building strategies. This automated approach not only saves time but also increases the effectiveness of link-building campaigns.

AI-Driven Tools and Techniques in SEO

Several AI-driven tools and techniques are transforming the SEO landscape. These tools utilize machine learning algorithms to analyze data and provide actionable insights that can enhance SEO strategies. Some of the most notable tools and techniques include:

1. AI-Powered Keyword Research Tools: **Tools like Ahrefs, SEMrush, and Moz use AI to analyze search queries, competition, and user intent. These tools provide detailed keyword analysis, helping marketers identify high-potential keywords and optimize their content accordingly.**

2. Content Optimization Tools: AI-driven content optimization tools like Clearscope and MarketMuse analyze top-performing content in a niche and provide recommendations on keywords, content structure, and readability. These tools ensure that content is both user-friendly and optimized for search engines.

3. Predictive Analytics: Predictive analytics tools use machine learning algorithms to forecast trends and user behavior. By analyzing historical data, these tools can predict future search trends, helping marketers stay ahead of the competition and create content that meets future demand.

4. Voice Search Optimization: With the rise of voice assistants like Siri, Alexa, and Google Assistant, optimizing for voice search is becoming increasingly important. AI can analyze voice search queries and help marketers optimize their content for natural language and conversational keywords.

5. AI Chatbots: AI-powered chatbots can enhance user experience by providing instant responses to user queries. These chatbots can also collect valuable data on user behavior and preferences, which can inform SEO strategies and content creation.

Future Trends in SEO and AI

The integration of AI and SEO is still in its early stages, and the future holds immense potential for further advancements. As AI technology continues to evolve, it is expected to drive several key trends in the SEO landscape.

One such trend is the increased emphasis on user experience. Search engines are likely to place even greater importance on UX, making it essential for marketers to leverage AI to enhance their websites' usability, speed, and accessibility. AI-driven personalization and recommendation engines will play a crucial role in providing a tailored user experience that meets individual needs and preferences.

Another emerging trend is the growth of visual and video search. With the advent of technologies like Google Lens and advanced image recognition, optimizing for visual search will become a critical component of SEO. AI can analyze visual content and provide recommendations on optimizing images and videos for search engines.

Furthermore, as AI algorithms become more sophisticated, they will be able to understand and process complex search queries with greater accuracy. This will lead to a more nuanced understanding of user intent, allowing marketers to create highly targeted and relevant content.

The rise of AI in SEO also underscores the importance of ethical considerations. As AI algorithms analyze vast amounts of data, it is crucial to ensure data privacy and transparency. Marketers must be mindful of ethical considerations and adhere to best practices in data collection and usage.

Conclusion

The integration of SEO and AI represents a transformative shift in digital marketing. By leveraging AI's data processing capabilities and predictive analytics, marketers can enhance their SEO strategies, improve user experience, and achieve higher search engine rankings. AI-driven tools and techniques are already making a significant impact, from advanced keyword research and content optimization to personalized user experiences and link building.

As AI technology continues to evolve, it will drive new trends and opportunities in the SEO landscape. Marketers who embrace AI and integrate it into their SEO strategies will be well-positioned to stay ahead of the competition and achieve long-term success. Understanding the synergy between SEO and AI is not just advantageous but essential for any digital marketer aiming to thrive in the ever-evolving digital landscape.

Chapter 3. Advanced Search Engine Optimization (SEO) Techniques

Introduction

In the dynamic realm of digital marketing, staying ahead requires more than just understanding the basics of SEO. As search engines evolve, so do the strategies needed to ensure optimal visibility and ranking. This chapter delves into advanced SEO techniques, highlighting both on-page and off-page strategies, and the burgeoning role of artificial intelligence in enhancing SEO performance.

On-Page SEO Strategies

On-page SEO refers to the optimization of individual web pages to rank higher and earn more relevant traffic in search engines. This involves meticulous attention to the content and HTML source code of a page, rather than external links and other external signals.

1. Content Quality and User Intent

In the age of sophisticated algorithms, high-quality content that satisfies user intent is paramount. Search engines like Google prioritize content that provides genuine value, answers user queries comprehensively, and is both engaging and relevant. To achieve this, it's essential to conduct thorough keyword research to understand what users are searching for and tailor content to meet these needs. Long-form content often performs better, as it allows for more in-depth exploration of topics, but it must be well-structured and easily readable.

2. Semantic SEO

Semantic SEO is about optimizing content for the true intent behind a user's search query rather than just focusing on specific keywords. This involves using related terms and phrases, understanding the context of queries, and providing comprehensive information. Implementing structured data markup (schema.org) can help search engines understand the content's context, enhancing the chances of appearing in rich snippets and improving overall visibility.

3. Technical SEO

Technical SEO ensures that a website meets the technical requirements of modern search engines. This includes improving site speed, ensuring mobile-friendliness, creating an XML sitemap, and using robots.txt to manage crawler access. Page speed is crucial; even a one-second delay can significantly impact bounce rates and user satisfaction. Tools like Google PageSpeed Insights can help identify and rectify issues slowing down your site.

4. On-Page Elements Optimization

Title tags, meta descriptions, header tags, and image alt text are critical components of on-page SEO. Title tags should be compelling and include target keywords, but remain concise. Meta descriptions, while not a direct ranking factor, influence click-through rates and should accurately summarize the page content. Header tags (H1, H2, H3, etc.) structure content and make it easier for both users and search engines to navigate. Optimizing image alt text helps with accessibility and provides additional opportunities to include keywords.

5. Internal Linking

A robust internal linking strategy helps distribute page authority across your site and guides users and search engines to your most important pages. Effective internal linking improves the overall site architecture, making it easier for search engines to crawl and index your site, and it enhances the user experience by providing additional value and context.

Off-Page SEO Strategies

Off-page SEO encompasses actions taken outside of your own website to impact your rankings within search engine results pages (SERPs). This is driven by factors such as backlinks, social signals, and other external indicators of website authority and popularity.

1. Backlink Building

Building high-quality backlinks remains a cornerstone of off-page SEO. Backlinks from authoritative and relevant websites signal to search engines that your site is trustworthy and valuable. Techniques for acquiring backlinks include guest blogging, influencer outreach, broken link building, and leveraging PR (Public Relations) efforts to get featured in reputable publications. The focus should be on quality over quantity, as low-quality links can harm your site's credibility and ranking.

2. Social Media Engagement

Social media platforms are powerful tools for enhancing your off-page SEO efforts. While social signals themselves are not direct ranking factors, they influence visibility and drive traffic to your site. Engaging content that resonates with your audience can lead to shares, likes, and comments, expanding your reach and potentially earning natural backlinks. Building a strong presence on platforms like Facebook, X (Twitter), LinkedIn, and Instagram can amplify your content and brand visibility.

3. Influencer Collaborations

Collaborating with influencers in your industry can significantly boost your off-page SEO. Influencers have established credibility and large followings, and their endorsements can drive traffic and generate valuable backlinks. Identifying and building relationships with influencers who align with your brand values and target audience can lead to mutually beneficial collaborations, enhancing your online presence and authority.

4. Online Reviews and Reputation Management

Positive online reviews and a strong reputation can impact your local SEO and overall online credibility. Encouraging satisfied customers to leave reviews on platforms like Google My Business, Yelp, and industry-specific review sites can improve your visibility and attract potential customers. Responding to reviews, both positive and negative, demonstrates your commitment to customer satisfaction and helps build trust with your audience.

5. Community Engagement and Forums

Participating in online communities and forums relevant to your industry can help establish your authority and generate traffic to your site. Providing valuable insights and answers to questions on platforms like Reddit, Quora, and industry-specific forums can position you as an expert and attract visitors to your site. Including links to your content when relevant and helpful can also contribute to your backlink profile.

Leveraging AI for Improved SEO Performance

Artificial Intelligence (AI) is revolutionizing SEO by providing advanced tools and techniques to optimize content, analyze data, and enhance user experience. AI-driven SEO tools can automate routine tasks, offer deep insights, and predict trends, allowing marketers to stay ahead of the curve.

1. AI-Powered Content Creation and Optimization

AI tools like GPT-4 and other natural language processing models can generate high-quality content, suggest relevant topics, and optimize existing content for better performance. These tools can analyze user intent, search patterns, and competitor content to provide data-driven recommendations for creating content that resonates with your audience. Additionally, AI can help identify content gaps and opportunities for improvement, ensuring your content remains relevant and competitive.

2. Predictive Analytics and Trend Analysis

AI can analyze vast amounts of data to predict trends and identify emerging topics in your industry. By leveraging predictive analytics, marketers can anticipate changes in user behavior, search patterns, and market demands, allowing them to adjust their SEO strategies proactively. Tools like Google Trends and AI-powered analytics platforms can provide valuable insights into search volume, seasonality, and keyword performance, guiding content creation and optimization efforts.

3. Automated SEO Audits and Monitoring

AI-driven SEO tools can conduct comprehensive site audits, identifying technical issues, on-page optimization opportunities, and backlink quality. Automated audits can save time and ensure that your site remains in optimal condition. Continuous monitoring tools powered by AI can alert you to any changes in site performance, keyword rankings, and backlink profile, allowing for timely interventions and adjustments to your SEO strategy.

4. Enhanced User Experience with AI

AI can significantly enhance user experience by personalizing content, improving site navigation, and providing real-time support. AI-powered chatbots and virtual assistants can engage with visitors, answer queries, and guide them through their journey, improving user satisfaction and retention. Personalization algorithms can deliver tailored content and recommendations based on user behavior and preferences, increasing engagement and conversion rates.

5. Voice Search Optimization

The rise of voice-activated devices and virtual assistants like Siri, Alexa, and Google Assistant has transformed search behavior. Optimizing for voice search involves understanding natural language queries, focusing on conversational keywords, and providing concise and direct answers. AI can analyze voice search patterns and suggest optimization strategies to ensure your content is easily discoverable through voice queries.

Conclusion

Advanced SEO techniques are essential for navigating the competitive landscape of digital marketing. By combining sophisticated on-page and off-page strategies with the power of AI, marketers can enhance their site's visibility, attract relevant traffic, and achieve sustainable growth. Continuous adaptation and leveraging innovative tools and technologies will ensure that your SEO efforts remain effective and aligned with evolving search engine algorithms and user behaviors.

Chapter 4. Maximizing Search Engine Marketing (SEM)

Introduction

Search Engine Marketing (SEM) has become an essential component of digital marketing strategies. SEM involves the use of paid advertising on search engines to increase visibility and drive traffic to websites. It's a powerful tool that allows businesses to reach potential customers at the precise moment they are searching for products or services. This chapter delves into the intricacies of SEM, exploring paid search strategies, best practices, and the integration of SEO and SEM for optimal results.

Understanding Search Engine Marketing

At its core, SEM encompasses all efforts to promote a website on search engines through paid advertising. Unlike Search Engine Optimization (SEO), which focuses on improving organic search results, SEM relies on paid placements, typically through pay-per-click (PPC) advertising. The most popular platform for SEM is Google Ads, though other search engines like Bing and Yahoo also offer paid advertising options.

Paid Search Strategies

A successful SEM campaign begins with a well-thought-out strategy. Here are some critical components of effective paid search strategies.

1. Keyword Research and Selection

The foundation of any SEM campaign is keyword research. Identifying the right keywords involves understanding what terms potential customers use to search for your products or services. Tools like Google Keyword Planner, SEMrush, and Ahrefs can help in discovering high-volume and relevant keywords. It's essential to focus on a mix of short-tail (broad) and long-tail (specific) keywords to capture a wide range of search queries.

2. Ad Creation and Optimization

Creating compelling ads is crucial for attracting clicks. Ads should be relevant, engaging, and aligned with the user's search intent. A well-crafted ad includes a catchy headline, a concise description, and a strong call-to-action (CTA). It's also important to use ad extensions, such as site links, callouts, and structured snippets, to provide additional information and improve ad visibility.

Regularly testing and optimizing ads is vital. A/B testing different versions of ad copy can help determine what resonates best with the audience. Metrics like click-through rate (CTR), conversion rate, and quality score should be monitored to gauge performance and make necessary adjustments.

A/B testing is a method of comparing two versions of a webpage or app to determine which one performs better based on user responses and behavior. *Click-through rate (CTR)* is the ratio of users who click on a specific link to the total number of users who view a webpage, email, or advertisement, expressed as a percentage. *Conversion rate* is the percentage of users who take a desired action (such as making a purchase or signing up for a newsletter) out of the total number of users who visit a webpage or app. *Quality score* is a metric used by search engines to measure the relevance and quality of keywords and ads, influencing the cost and effectiveness of pay-per-click (PPC) advertising campaigns.

3. Bid Management

Bid management is a critical aspect of SEM. It involves setting the maximum amount you're willing to pay for a click on your ad. Effective bid management ensures you're getting the best return on investment (ROI) without overspending. There are various bidding strategies available, such as manual bidding, automated bidding, and portfolio bidding. Each has its advantages and should be chosen based on campaign goals and budget.

4. Landing Page Optimization

Driving traffic to a website is only half the battle; converting that traffic is equally important. This is where landing page optimization comes into play. A well-designed landing page should be relevant to the ad that brought the user there, provide a clear value proposition, and have a strong CTA. The page should load quickly, be mobile-friendly, and offer a seamless user experience.

Call to Action (CTA) is a prompt on a webpage, advertisement, or piece of content that encourages the audience to take a specific action, such as "Buy Now," "Sign Up," or "Learn More."

Best Practices for SEM

To maximize the effectiveness of SEM campaigns, it's essential to follow best practices that enhance performance and drive better results.

1. Continuous Monitoring and Adjustment

SEM is not a set-it-and-forget-it strategy. Continuous monitoring of campaign performance is crucial. Analyzing data regularly helps identify what's working and what's not. Metrics such as CTR, conversion rate, cost-per-click (CPC), and ROI should be closely watched. Based on these insights, adjustments can be made to keywords, ad copy, bids, and landing pages to improve performance.

Cost-per-click (CPC) is the amount an advertiser pays each time a user clicks on their online ad. *Return on Investment* (ROI) is a measure of the profitability of an investment, calculated as the ratio of net profit to the cost of the investment, often expressed as a percentage.

2. Leveraging Negative Keywords

Negative keywords are terms that you don't want your ads to show for. Adding negative keywords to your campaigns helps prevent your ads from appearing in irrelevant searches, thereby saving budget and improving the quality of traffic. For example, if you sell premium software, you might add "free" as a negative keyword to avoid attracting users looking for free solutions.

3. Utilizing Ad Extensions

Ad extensions enhance the visibility and effectiveness of your ads. By providing additional information, such as phone numbers, locations, and links to specific pages on your website, ad extensions make your ads more compelling and increase the chances of a click. They can also improve your ad's quality score, leading to better ad placements at lower costs.

4. Retargeting and Remarketing

Retargeting, also known as remarketing, is a powerful tactic that involves targeting users who have previously visited your website but did not convert. By showing these users tailored ads as they browse other sites or use social media, you can remind them of your products or services and encourage them to return and complete a purchase. Retargeting campaigns often yield high conversion rates as they focus on users already familiar with your brand.

Integrating SEO and SEM for Optimal Results

While SEM focuses on paid search, SEO aims to improve organic search rankings. Integrating both strategies can lead to more comprehensive and effective search engine marketing efforts. Here's how to achieve optimal results by combining SEO and SEM.

1. Keyword Synergy

SEO and SEM both rely on keyword research. By aligning the keywords targeted in both strategies, you can create a unified approach that maximizes visibility. Use insights from your SEM campaigns to inform your SEO strategy and vice versa. For instance, if a particular keyword performs well in paid search, consider optimizing your website's content for that keyword to improve organic rankings.

2. Shared Data Insights

Both SEO and SEM generate valuable data that can be shared to enhance overall performance. SEM campaigns provide immediate feedback on keyword performance, user behavior, and ad effectiveness. This data can inform SEO efforts by highlighting which keywords and topics are worth focusing on. Conversely, long-term SEO data can offer insights into which keywords maintain high relevance and drive consistent traffic, helping refine SEM strategies.

3. Enhanced Brand Presence

Combining SEO and SEM can significantly enhance brand presence on search engine results pages (SERPs). By occupying both paid and organic listings, you increase the likelihood of users seeing and clicking on your links. This dual presence builds credibility and reinforces your brand message, making users more likely to choose your site over competitors.

4. Holistic User Experience

A seamless user experience is essential for both SEO and SEM. Ensure that your website provides a consistent and positive experience for users, regardless of how they arrive - whether through a paid ad or an organic search result. This includes optimizing site speed, mobile responsiveness, and user-friendly navigation. A holistic approach improves the chances of converting visitors into customers.

Conclusion

Maximizing Search Engine Marketing requires a strategic and integrated approach. By employing effective paid search strategies, adhering to best practices, and integrating

SEO and SEM efforts, businesses can significantly enhance their visibility, drive targeted traffic, and achieve better overall results. Continuous monitoring, data-driven adjustments, and a focus on user experience are key to sustaining and improving SEM performance. As the digital marketing landscape evolves, staying informed and adaptable will ensure your SEM campaigns remain competitive and effective.

Chapter 5. Harnessing the Power of SEMrush

Introduction

In the fast-paced world of digital marketing, tools that offer comprehensive insights and capabilities are invaluable. SEMrush stands out as one such tool, providing a suite of features designed to bolster both SEO (Search Engine Optimization) and SEM (Search Engine Marketing) efforts. This article delves into the extensive functionalities of SEMrush, offering an in-depth guide on how to leverage its power to enhance your digital marketing strategies. Additionally, we'll explore case studies and best practices to illustrate its impact in real-world scenarios.

Understanding SEMrush

SEMrush is an all-in-one digital marketing platform that provides solutions for SEO, PPC (Pay-Per-Click), content marketing, social media, and competitive research. By offering a comprehensive range of tools, SEMrush enables marketers to improve their online visibility and discover marketing insights.

Getting Started with SEMrush

To begin using SEMrush, you need to set up an account and configure your dashboard. The dashboard serves as the central hub where you can manage projects, track keyword rankings, and analyze competitors. Once your account is set up, it's crucial to familiarize yourself with the primary tools and reports that SEMrush offers.

Keyword Research and Analysis

One of the core functions of SEMrush is keyword research. The Keyword Magic Tool is particularly powerful, allowing users to generate a list of potential keywords for their campaigns. By inputting a seed keyword, you can explore thousands of related keywords along with their search volume, keyword difficulty, and competitive density.

Analyzing keyword data helps in identifying high-potential keywords that can drive traffic to your site. SEMrush also provides insights into keyword trends, which can be useful for staying ahead of market changes. By understanding which keywords your competitors are ranking for, you can refine your strategy and target untapped opportunities.

On-Page SEO and Site Audits

On-page SEO is critical for improving your website's visibility on search engines. SEMrush's Site Audit tool is designed to evaluate your website's health and identify issues that might be affecting its performance. The audit report highlights errors, warnings, and notices, along with recommendations for improvement.

Addressing issues such as broken links, duplicate content, and missing meta tags can significantly enhance your site's SEO. The On-Page SEO Checker tool further provides actionable insights by analyzing your pages and suggesting optimization ideas based on your target keywords and competitors.

Competitor Analysis

Understanding your competitors' strategies is essential for gaining a competitive edge. SEMrush's Competitive Research Toolkit offers a wealth of information about your competitors' online activities. The Domain Overview report provides a snapshot of their organic and paid search performance, while the Traffic Analytics tool reveals their website traffic sources and user behavior.

By analyzing competitor data, you can uncover their top-performing keywords, backlinks, and content strategies. This information can inform your own marketing efforts, helping you to develop more effective campaigns and identify gaps in the market.

Content Marketing Insights

Content is at the heart of digital marketing, and SEMrush offers several tools to enhance your content strategy. The Topic Research tool helps generate content ideas by providing a list of subtopics and related questions based on your main keyword. This ensures your content is relevant and addresses the needs of your audience.

The SEO Content Template tool offers guidelines for creating content that is optimized for search engines. By analyzing the top-ranking pages for your target keywords, it suggests the optimal length, readability, and use of keywords for your content. Additionally, the Brand Monitoring tool tracks mentions of your brand across the web, helping you measure the impact of your content and PR efforts.

Link Building Strategies

Backlinks remain a crucial factor in search engine ranking algorithms. SEMrush's Backlink Analytics and Backlink Audit tools offer comprehensive insights into your backlink profile and opportunities for link building. The Backlink Analytics tool provides data on referring domains, anchor texts, and link types, helping you understand your existing backlinks.

The Backlink Gap tool identifies backlink opportunities by comparing your backlink profile with those of your competitors. This allows you to discover potential sites for outreach and link acquisition. Furthermore, the Backlink Audit tool helps you identify toxic backlinks that could harm your site's SEO, allowing you to disavow them and maintain a healthy backlink profile.

PPC and Advertising Research

SEMrush is not limited to SEO; it also offers robust tools for managing and optimizing PPC campaigns. The Advertising Research tool provides insights into your competitors' ad strategies, including their top keywords, ad copy, and landing pages. This information can help you craft more effective PPC campaigns and improve your ad performance.

The Keyword Gap tool allows you to compare your PPC keywords with those of your competitors, identifying gaps and opportunities. By leveraging these insights, you can refine your keyword targeting and bidding strategies to maximize ROI.

Case Studies and Best Practices

To illustrate the power of SEMrush, let's examine a few case studies and best practices from businesses that have successfully harnessed its capabilities.

Case Study 1: E-commerce SEO Success

An e-commerce company specializing in outdoor gear used SEMrush to revamp its SEO strategy. By conducting comprehensive keyword research, they identified high-potential keywords related to their products. The On-Page SEO Checker helped them optimize product pages, leading to a 30% increase in organic traffic within six months. Additionally, the Backlink Audit tool enabled them to clean up their backlink profile, further boosting their search rankings.

Case Study 2: Content Marketing Transformation

A tech blog leveraged SEMrush's content marketing tools to enhance its editorial strategy. Using the Topic Research tool, they identified trending topics and frequently asked questions in their niche. This led to the creation of highly relevant and engaging content that resonated with their audience. The SEO Content Template guided them in optimizing their articles, resulting in a 25% increase in page views and a 15% rise in user engagement.

Best Practice: Continuous Monitoring and Optimization

One of the best practices for using SEMrush is to continuously monitor your performance and make data-driven optimizations. Regular site audits and keyword tracking help you stay on top of changes and identify new opportunities. By consistently analyzing competitor data, you can adapt your strategies and maintain a competitive edge.

Best Practice: Leveraging Multiple Tools

To maximize the benefits of SEMrush, it's important to leverage its full suite of tools. Combining insights from keyword research, site audits, competitor analysis, and content marketing can provide a holistic view of your digital marketing efforts. This integrated approach ensures that all aspects of your strategy are aligned and optimized for success.

Conclusion

Harnessing the power of SEMrush requires a deep understanding of its diverse tools and how they can be applied to your specific marketing goals. From keyword research and on-page SEO to competitor analysis and content marketing, SEMrush offers comprehensive solutions for enhancing your digital marketing strategies. By following best practices and learning from successful case studies, you can unlock the full potential of SEMrush and achieve significant improvements in your online visibility and performance. As the digital landscape continues to evolve, SEMrush remains an indispensable ally for marketers aiming to stay ahead of the competition and drive sustainable growth.

Chapter 6. Leveraging Google Analytics for Insights and Growth

Introduction

In the ever-evolving landscape of digital marketing, data is king. The ability to collect, analyze, and act upon data is crucial for businesses aiming to thrive online. One of the most powerful tools at the disposal of digital marketers is Google Analytics. This robust platform provides a wealth of insights that can drive strategic decisions and fuel growth. This chapter delves into understanding and utilizing Google Analytics, and how its data can be harnessed to craft and refine digital marketing strategies.

Understanding Google Analytics

Google Analytics is a free web analytics service offered by Google that tracks and reports website traffic. Launched in 2005, it has become the most widely used web analytics service on the internet. At its core, Google Analytics collects data through a JavaScript code embedded in the webpages of a site. This code records various user activities, such as page views, clicks, and transactions, and sends this data back to Google's servers for processing.

The data collected by Google Analytics is vast and can be segmented into various categories such as user demographics, behavior, acquisition channels, and conversion metrics. Understanding these categories is the first step in leveraging Google Analytics effectively.

Utilizing Google Analytics

The power of Google Analytics lies not just in the collection of data, but in the insights that can be derived from it. Here's how businesses can utilize Google Analytics to its full potential.

1. Setting Up and Configuring Google Analytics

Before diving into the data, it's crucial to set up Google Analytics correctly. This involves creating a Google Analytics account, adding properties (websites or apps), and generating the tracking code. Proper configuration is essential to ensure accurate data collection. This includes setting up filters to exclude internal traffic, defining goals that align with business objectives, and linking Google Analytics with other Google tools like Google Ads and Search Console for a more comprehensive view of performance.

2. Navigating the Google Analytics Interface

The Google Analytics interface can be overwhelming at first glance. It consists of several sections, each providing different types of data. The 'Home' dashboard gives a high-level overview of key metrics. The 'Real-Time' reports show live user activity on the site. 'Audience' reports provide insights into the characteristics of the site visitors, including demographics, interests, and behavior. 'Acquisition' reports reveal how users are arriving at the site, whether through organic search, social media, or paid campaigns. 'Behavior' reports show how users interact with the site, and 'Conversions' track goal completions and e-commerce transactions.

Using Data to Drive Digital Marketing Strategies

Data is only as valuable as the actions it informs. Here's how Google Analytics data can be used to drive digital marketing strategies.

1. Identifying Audience Demographics and Interests

Understanding who your audience is can significantly impact your marketing strategies. Google Analytics provides detailed insights into the demographics and interests of your site visitors. This information can help tailor content and advertisements to better match the preferences of your target audience. For instance, if the data reveals that a significant portion of the audience is interested in technology, a business might focus on creating tech-related content and targeting tech enthusiasts in their ad campaigns.

2. Analyzing User Behavior

Analyzing how users interact with your site can uncover areas for improvement. Google Analytics shows which pages are most popular, how long users stay on each page, and the paths they take through the site. High bounce rates on specific pages might indicate that the content or user experience needs enhancement. By understanding user behavior, businesses can optimize their websites to improve engagement and reduce bounce rates.

3. Tracking Acquisition Channels

Knowing how users find your site is crucial for effective marketing. Google Analytics breaks down traffic into channels such as organic search, paid search, direct traffic, social media, and referrals. By analyzing these channels, businesses can determine which marketing efforts are driving the most traffic and conversions. For instance, if organic search is a major traffic source, investing in SEO efforts can yield significant returns. Conversely, if paid search is underperforming, it may be necessary to refine ad targeting or budget allocation.

4. Measuring Campaign Performance

For businesses running multiple marketing campaigns, tracking performance is essential. Google Analytics allows marketers to set up campaign tracking using UTM parameters (tags added to URLs to track the effectiveness of online marketing campaigns through Google Analytics). This enables the precise measurement of traffic and conversions from different campaigns, sources, mediums, and content variations. By analyzing this data, businesses can identify the most effective campaigns and adjust strategies to maximize ROI.

5. Conversion Tracking and Goal Setting

One of the most powerful features of Google Analytics is its ability to track conversions. Conversions can be anything from completing a purchase to filling out a contact form. By setting up goals in Google Analytics, businesses can measure how well their site fulfills target objectives. Goal tracking provides valuable insights into the customer journey and highlights any obstacles that might prevent users from converting. This information is crucial for optimizing the site and marketing efforts to improve conversion rates.

6. E-commerce Tracking

For e-commerce businesses, Google Analytics offers enhanced e-commerce tracking capabilities. This feature provides detailed insights into product performance, sales trends, and customer behavior. Businesses can track metrics such as product impressions, add-to-cart actions, and purchase completions. This data can inform inventory decisions, marketing promotions, and overall business strategy.

7. Leveraging Custom Reports and Dashboards

Google Analytics allows users to create custom reports and dashboards tailored to their specific needs. This customization enables businesses to focus on the most relevant metrics and data points. Custom dashboards provide a quick snapshot of key performance indicators (KPIs), making it easier to monitor progress and make informed decisions. For example, an e-commerce site might create a dashboard that tracks daily sales, average order value, and cart abandonment rates.

8. Enhancing User Experience

A positive user experience is critical for retaining visitors and driving conversions. Google Analytics provides insights into various aspects of user experience, such as site speed, mobile usability, and navigation paths. By identifying and addressing issues that hinder the user experience, businesses can improve site performance and increase user satisfaction. For instance, if the data shows that mobile users have a higher bounce rate, optimizing the mobile site design and functionality could enhance the overall experience.

9. Implementing A/B Testing

A/B testing, or split testing, is a method of comparing two versions of a webpage or app to determine which performs better. Google Analytics can be integrated with Google Optimize, a tool that facilitates A/B testing. By running experiments and analyzing the results, businesses can make data-driven decisions to improve site elements such as headlines, images, and calls to action. A/B testing helps in identifying the most effective variations that drive higher engagement and conversions.

Leveraging Advanced Features

Google Analytics offers several advanced features that can provide deeper insights and more granular control over data analysis.

1. Segmentation

Segmentation allows businesses to isolate and analyze specific subsets of data. By creating segments based on various criteria such as user behavior, traffic source, or demographic information, businesses can gain more detailed insights. For instance, analyzing the behavior of returning visitors versus new visitors can reveal patterns that inform marketing strategies. Segmentation helps in understanding different audience segments and tailoring marketing efforts accordingly.

2. Attribution Modeling

Attribution modeling is the process of assigning credit to various touchpoints in the customer journey. Google Analytics offers several attribution models, such as last-click, first-click, and linear attribution. Understanding which touchpoints contribute most to conversions can help businesses allocate marketing resources more effectively. For example, if a particular social media campaign is identified as a key driver of conversions, increasing investment in that channel could yield better results.

3. Cohort Analysis

Cohort analysis involves studying the behavior of groups of users who share a common characteristic, such as the date of acquisition (the specific date when users first interact with a service, or platform). This analysis can provide insights into user retention and engagement over time. By understanding how different cohorts behave, businesses can identify trends and optimize their marketing efforts to improve user retention and lifetime value.

4. Multi-Channel Funnels

Multi-channel funnels in Google Analytics show how different marketing channels work together to drive conversions. This feature provides a more holistic view of the customer journey, highlighting the interplay between various channels. By analyzing multi-channel funnels, businesses can identify the most effective channel combinations and optimize their marketing strategies to ensure a cohesive and efficient approach.

Conclusion

Google Analytics is an indispensable tool for digital marketers seeking to harness the power of data for insights and growth. From understanding audience demographics to tracking campaign performance and optimizing user experience, the insights provided by Google Analytics can inform and refine digital marketing strategies. By leveraging its full range of features, businesses can make data-driven decisions that drive traffic, increase engagement, and boost conversions. In the dynamic world of digital marketing, Google Analytics stands out as a vital resource for achieving sustained growth and success.

Chapter 7. Market Research in the Digital World

Introduction

Market research has long been the backbone of strategic business decisions, guiding companies on what consumers want, how they behave, and what drives their purchasing decisions. In the digital age, the methodologies and tools available for conducting market research have evolved dramatically. The digital world offers a plethora of data sources, advanced analytical tools, and innovative techniques that allow businesses to understand their market and customers with unprecedented depth and precision. This chapter explores the intricacies of market research in the digital world, focusing on techniques for gathering and analyzing digital data and the transformative role of artificial intelligence (AI) in enhancing market research insights.

Techniques for Gathering Digital Data

The digital landscape provides an expansive array of data collection techniques that are both diverse and sophisticated. These techniques leverage the internet, social media, mobile applications, and other digital platforms to gather rich and actionable data.

1. Web Analytics: Web analytics tools like Google Analytics provide comprehensive insights into website traffic, user behavior, and conversion rates. By tracking metrics such as page views, session duration, bounce rates, and user demographics, businesses can gain a deep understanding of how users interact with their websites.

This data is invaluable for optimizing website design, content, and marketing strategies to enhance user engagement and drive conversions.

2. Social Media Monitoring: Social media platforms are a goldmine of consumer data. Tools like Hootsuite, Sprout Social, and Brandwatch allow businesses to monitor conversations, track mentions, and analyze sentiment across various social media channels. By understanding what customers are saying about their brand, competitors, and industry, businesses can identify trends, measure brand sentiment, and engage with their audience more effectively.

3. Surveys and Polls: Online surveys and polls are traditional market research methods that have been adapted for the digital age. Platforms like SurveyMonkey, Qualtrics, and Google Forms enable businesses to create and distribute surveys quickly and efficiently. These tools provide detailed analytics on responses, allowing businesses to gather quantitative data on customer preferences, satisfaction levels, and market needs.

4. Customer Feedback and Reviews: Online reviews and customer feedback are critical sources of qualitative data. Websites like Yelp, TripAdvisor, and Amazon provide a wealth of information about customer experiences and perceptions. Analyzing this feedback helps businesses identify strengths and weaknesses, improve products and services, and build stronger customer relationships.

5. Behavioral Tracking: Digital platforms enable the tracking of user behavior across websites, apps, and other online channels. This includes tracking clicks, scrolls, mouse movements, and other interactions. Tools like Hotjar and Crazy Egg offer heatmaps and session recordings that reveal how users navigate digital interfaces, providing

insights into user experience and behavior patterns. *Heatmaps* are visual representations of data that use color coding to show the intensity of user interactions, such as clicks, scrolls, or mouse movements, on a webpage, helping to identify areas of high and low engagement.

Analyzing Digital Data

Once data is collected, the next step is analysis. Analyzing digital data involves transforming raw data into meaningful insights that can inform business decisions. This process requires robust analytical tools and techniques.

1. Data Cleaning and Preparation: **Before analysis, it's crucial to clean and prepare the data. This involves removing duplicates, correcting errors, and standardizing formats. Tools like Excel, R, and Python libraries (e.g., Pandas) are commonly used for data cleaning and preparation. Proper data preparation ensures that the analysis is accurate and reliable.**

2. Descriptive Analytics: **Descriptive analytics involves summarizing and visualizing data to understand what has happened. This can include calculating averages, percentages, and frequencies, as well as creating charts and graphs. Tools like Tableau, Power BI, and Google Data Studio are powerful for visualizing data and identifying patterns and trends.**

3. Predictive Analytics: **Predictive analytics uses historical data to forecast future outcomes. Techniques such as regression analysis, time series analysis, and machine learning algorithms are employed to make predictions about customer behavior, market trends, and sales performance. Predictive analytics enables businesses to anticipate changes and make proactive decisions.**

4. Sentiment Analysis: Sentiment analysis involves analyzing text data to determine the emotional tone behind words. This technique is particularly useful for understanding customer sentiment in social media posts, reviews, and feedback. Natural language processing (NLP) tools and libraries, such as TextBlob and VADER, help businesses gauge public sentiment and adjust their strategies accordingly.

5. Cohort Analysis: Cohort analysis involves grouping users based on shared characteristics or behaviors and analyzing these groups over time. This technique helps businesses understand how different segments of customers behave and how their behavior changes over time. Cohort analysis is useful for identifying trends, improving customer retention, and tailoring marketing efforts to specific segments.

Using AI to Enhance Market Research Insights

Artificial intelligence (AI) is revolutionizing market research by providing advanced tools and techniques for data analysis. AI enhances the accuracy, efficiency, and depth of market research insights, enabling businesses to make more informed decisions.

1. Automated Data Collection: AI-powered tools can automate the process of data collection, saving time and reducing the risk of human error. For example, web scraping tools can automatically gather data from websites, while chatbots can collect customer feedback in real-time. Automation allows businesses to collect larger volumes of data more efficiently.

2. Machine Learning: Machine learning algorithms can analyze vast amounts of data to identify patterns and make predictions. These algorithms can be used for tasks such as customer segmentation, churn prediction, and recommendation systems. *Churn prediction* is the process of identifying which customers are likely to stop using a product or service within a given time period, using data analysis and machine learning techniques to anticipate and mitigate customer attrition. Machine learning enhances the ability to uncover hidden insights and make data-driven decisions.

3. Natural Language Processing (NLP): NLP enables computers to understand and interpret human language. In market research, NLP can be used to analyze text data from social media, reviews, and surveys. By understanding the context and sentiment of the text, businesses can gain deeper insights into customer opinions and preferences.

4. Image and Video Analysis: AI can analyze images and videos to extract valuable information. For instance, facial recognition technology can assess customer emotions in video feedback, while image recognition can analyze product images shared on social media. This type of analysis provides a richer understanding of customer experiences and perceptions.

5. Real-Time Analytics: AI enables real-time data analysis, allowing businesses to respond quickly to changes in the market. Real-time analytics tools can monitor social media activity, track website performance, and analyze customer behavior as it happens. This immediacy allows businesses to capitalize on emerging trends and address issues promptly.

6. Personalization: AI can personalize marketing efforts based on individual customer data. By analyzing customer behavior and preferences, AI can deliver personalized recommendations, content, and offers. Personalization enhances customer engagement and loyalty by providing a more tailored and relevant experience.

7. Voice and Chat Analysis: Voice recognition and chat analysis technologies can analyze customer interactions with voice assistants and chatbots. These technologies can identify customer needs, preferences, and pain points based on their conversations. This analysis helps businesses improve customer service and tailor their offerings to meet customer needs more effectively.

Challenges and Ethical Considerations

While digital market research offers numerous benefits, it also presents challenges and ethical considerations. One of the main challenges is data privacy. Collecting and analyzing large amounts of personal data raises concerns about how this data is used and protected. Businesses must comply with data protection regulations, such as the General Data Protection Regulation (GDPR) enacted by the European Union, and ensure that customer data is handled responsibly.

Another challenge is data quality. The accuracy and reliability of digital data can vary, and businesses must ensure that their data collection methods are robust and their analyses are sound. This requires investing in high-quality tools and training staff to handle digital data effectively.

Ethically, businesses must be transparent about their data collection practices and respect customer consent.

Customers should be informed about what data is being collected, how it will be used, and how they can opt-out if they choose. Maintaining trust and integrity is crucial for building strong customer relationships.

Conclusion

Market research in the digital world is a dynamic and multifaceted field that leverages advanced technologies and techniques to gather and analyze data. From web analytics and social media monitoring to AI-powered insights, digital market research provides businesses with the tools they need to understand their market and customers deeply. By embracing these technologies and methodologies, businesses can make more informed decisions, anticipate market changes, and create more effective marketing strategies. However, it is essential to navigate the challenges and ethical considerations associated with digital data to maintain trust and integrity in the market research process. As technology continues to evolve, the potential for digital market research to drive business success will only grow, making it an indispensable component of modern marketing strategies.

Chapter 8. Lead Generation in the Digital Age

Introduction

Lead generation is the process of attracting and converting prospects into potential customers who have shown interest in a company's product or service, typically through various marketing strategies and tactics. Lead generation has always been a critical component of business growth, but the digital age has revolutionized how companies attract and convert leads. With the proliferation of online tools, platforms, and technologies, businesses now have unprecedented opportunities to reach their target audience and nurture relationships that drive conversions. This chapter delves into the strategies and innovations that define lead generation in the digital era, highlighting the pivotal role of artificial intelligence (AI) in optimizing these processes.

Strategies for Attracting and Converting Leads

In the digital landscape, attracting and converting leads requires a multifaceted approach that integrates content marketing, social media engagement, search engine optimization (SEO), email marketing, and paid advertising. Each of these strategies plays a unique role in capturing the interest of potential customers and guiding them through the sales funnel.

1. Content Marketing

Content marketing remains at the forefront of digital lead generation. By creating valuable, relevant, and consistent content, businesses can attract and retain a clearly defined audience. Blog posts, whitepapers, eBooks, webinars, and videos are among the various content formats that can be used to engage prospects. *Whitepapers* are authoritative, in-depth reports or guides that address specific topics, issues, or problems, providing detailed information, insights, and solutions to help readers understand and make informed decisions. High-quality content not only establishes a brand's authority but also provides solutions to the problems faced by potential leads, thereby fostering trust and credibility.

To maximize the impact of content marketing, businesses must employ a strategic approach to content distribution. This involves leveraging multiple channels, including company websites, social media platforms, and email newsletters, to reach a broader audience. Additionally, incorporating strong calls-to-action (CTAs) within content can drive leads to take the next step, such as downloading a resource, signing up for a webinar, or requesting a consultation.

2. Social Media Engagement

Social media platforms are indispensable tools for lead generation, offering a direct line of communication between businesses and their target audience. By maintaining an active presence on platforms like Facebook, LinkedIn, X (Twitter), and Instagram, companies can engage with potential leads, share valuable content, and participate in relevant conversations.

Effective social media engagement goes beyond posting content. It involves listening to and interacting with followers, responding to comments and messages, and participating in industry-related groups and discussions.

Social media advertising also plays a crucial role in lead generation. Paid campaigns, particularly those using advanced targeting options, can reach specific demographics, interests, and behaviors, ensuring that marketing efforts are directed toward the most promising leads.

3. Search Engine Optimization (SEO)

SEO is a cornerstone of digital lead generation, as it enhances the visibility of a business in search engine results pages (SERPs). By optimizing website content for relevant keywords, improving site structure, and building high-quality backlinks, companies can attract organic traffic from search engines like Google.

An effective SEO strategy involves both on-page and off-page optimization. On-page optimization includes elements such as meta tags, header tags, and keyword placement, while off-page optimization focuses on building authority through backlinks from reputable sites. Local SEO is also essential for businesses targeting specific geographic regions, as it ensures visibility in local search results.

4. Email Marketing

Email marketing remains a powerful tool for nurturing leads and guiding them through the sales funnel. By collecting email addresses through lead magnets like free resources or newsletter sign-ups, businesses can build a database of potential customers. Regular email communication, tailored to the interests and behaviors of recipients, helps maintain engagement and keeps the brand top-of-mind.

Personalization is key to successful email marketing. By segmenting email lists based on demographics, past interactions, and purchase history, companies can send targeted messages that resonate with individual leads. Automated email workflows, such as welcome sequences and drip campaigns, further enhance the efficiency and effectiveness of email marketing efforts. *Drip campaigns are automated marketing strategies that send a series of pre-scheduled messages or content to prospects or customers over time, typically via email, to nurture leads and maintain engagement.*

5. Paid Advertising

Paid advertising, including pay-per-click (PPC) campaigns and social media ads, is a direct method of driving traffic and generating leads. Platforms like Google Ads and Facebook Ads offer sophisticated targeting options that allow businesses to reach specific audience segments based on demographics, interests, and behaviors.

To optimize paid advertising efforts, businesses must continually monitor and adjust their campaigns. This involves testing different ad creatives, headlines, and CTAs (call-to-actions), as well as analyzing performance metrics to identify what works best. Remarketing campaigns, which target users who have previously interacted with the brand, can also be highly effective in converting leads.

The Role of AI in Lead Generation

Artificial intelligence (AI) has emerged as a game-changer in the realm of lead generation, offering innovative solutions that enhance efficiency, personalization, and overall effectiveness. AI technologies, such as machine learning, natural language processing (NLP), and predictive analytics, are transforming how businesses identify, attract, and convert leads.

1. Predictive Analytics

Predictive analytics leverages AI to analyze vast amounts of data and predict future outcomes. In lead generation, this technology can identify patterns and trends that indicate which leads are most likely to convert. By scoring leads based on their likelihood to become customers, businesses can prioritize their efforts and allocate resources more effectively.

Predictive analytics also enables more accurate forecasting and decision-making. By understanding which marketing strategies and channels are most effective at different stages of the sales funnel, companies can refine their approaches and optimize their lead generation campaigns.

2. Chatbots and Virtual Assistants

AI-powered chatbots and virtual assistants are revolutionizing customer interaction and lead nurturing. These tools can engage with website visitors in real-time, answering questions, providing information, and guiding users through the sales process. By offering instant support, chatbots enhance the user experience and capture leads that might otherwise be lost.

NLP, or Natural Language Processing, is a field of artificial intelligence that focuses on the interaction between computers and humans through natural language, enabling machines to understand, interpret, and respond to human language in a meaningful way. Advanced chatbots utilize NLP to understand and respond to complex queries, making interactions more natural and effective. They can also collect valuable data about user preferences and behaviors, which can be used to personalize future interactions and marketing efforts.

3. Personalization and Segmentation

AI excels at processing and analyzing data to deliver highly personalized experiences. In lead generation, this capability is invaluable for tailoring marketing messages and content to individual leads based on their behavior, preferences, and demographics. AI-driven personalization ensures that potential customers receive relevant and engaging content, increasing the likelihood of conversion.

Segmentation is another area where AI proves beneficial. By automatically grouping leads based on various criteria, AI enables businesses to create targeted campaigns that resonate with specific audience segments. This level of precision enhances the effectiveness of marketing efforts and drives higher conversion rates.

4. Automated Workflows

AI-powered automation streamlines many aspects of lead generation, from initial contact to nurturing and conversion. Automated workflows can handle repetitive tasks such as sending follow-up emails, scheduling appointments, and tracking interactions. This not only saves time but also ensures consistent and timely communication with leads.

Marketing automation platforms, enhanced with AI, can trigger actions based on specific lead behaviors. For example, if a lead downloads a whitepaper, the system can automatically send a follow-up email with additional resources or an invitation to a webinar. These automated workflows keep leads engaged and move them closer to conversion.

5. Enhanced Data Insights

AI provides deeper insights into customer data, allowing businesses to understand their leads better and make more informed decisions. By analyzing data from various sources, AI can uncover hidden patterns and correlations that traditional methods might miss. This comprehensive understanding of lead behavior and preferences enables more effective targeting and personalized marketing strategies.

Moreover, AI can continuously learn and adapt based on new data, ensuring that lead generation strategies remain relevant and effective in an ever-changing digital landscape. This dynamic approach helps businesses stay ahead of the competition and respond to emerging trends and opportunities.

Conclusion

Lead generation in the digital age is a dynamic and multifaceted process that leverages a variety of strategies and technologies to attract and convert potential customers. Content marketing, social media engagement, SEO, email marketing, and paid advertising each play crucial roles in this ecosystem. The integration of artificial intelligence further enhances lead generation efforts by providing predictive analytics, personalized experiences, automated workflows, and deep data insights.

As businesses continue to navigate the complexities of the digital landscape, embracing these strategies and technologies will be essential for sustaining growth and achieving success. The ability to effectively generate and nurture leads in a digital world not only drives revenue but also builds lasting relationships with customers, fostering loyalty and advocacy in the long term.

Chapter 9. Content Marketing

Introduction

In the digital age, content marketing has emerged as a vital component of any effective digital marketing strategy. As businesses strive to capture the attention of their target audiences amidst the noise of countless online messages, content marketing offers a powerful way to connect, engage, and convert prospects into loyal customers. This chapter delves into the intricacies of content marketing, exploring its significance, the process of developing a content strategy, and the various types of content that play pivotal roles in a successful campaign.

The Importance of Content Marketing

Content marketing is the strategic approach of creating and distributing valuable, relevant, and consistent content to attract and retain a clearly defined audience. Unlike traditional advertising, which directly promotes products or services, content marketing aims to provide information that educates, entertains, or inspires. This approach builds trust and credibility, positioning the brand as an authority in its industry.

The benefits of content marketing are manifold. It helps improve brand awareness, drives organic traffic, boosts search engine rankings, and enhances customer engagement. Furthermore, it nurtures leads through the sales funnel, ultimately leading to higher conversion rates. As consumers increasingly seek authentic and informative content, businesses that excel in content marketing are better positioned to foster long-term relationships with their audiences.

Developing a Content Strategy

A successful content marketing campaign begins with a well-defined content strategy. This strategy serves as a roadmap, guiding the creation, distribution, and management of content to achieve specific business objectives. Developing a content strategy involves several key steps.

1. Define Goals and Objectives

The first step in crafting a content strategy is to establish clear goals and objectives. These may include increasing brand awareness, driving website traffic, generating leads, or enhancing customer retention. By setting measurable and achievable goals, businesses can align their content efforts with their overall marketing strategy.

2. Understand the Target Audience

A deep understanding of the target audience is crucial for creating content that resonates. Businesses should develop detailed buyer personas that encompass demographic information, preferences, pain points, and behavior patterns. *Pain points* are specific problems or challenges that customers or potential customers experience, which a business aims to address and solve through its products or services. This information helps tailor content to address the specific needs and interests of the audience.

3. Conduct a Content Audit

Before creating new content, it's essential to assess existing content. A content audit involves evaluating the performance of current content, identifying gaps, and determining which pieces can be repurposed or updated. This process ensures that resources are allocated efficiently and that the content aligns with the overall strategy.

4. Plan Content Topics and Formats

With a clear understanding of the audience and existing content, businesses can brainstorm content topics and formats. It's important to choose topics that align with the audience's interests and the brand's expertise. Additionally, diversifying content formats, such as blogs, videos, infographics, and podcasts, ensures a well-rounded approach that caters to different consumption preferences.

5. Create a Content Calendar

A content calendar is a crucial tool for organizing and scheduling content production and distribution. It helps maintain consistency, ensures timely publication, and allows for better coordination among team members. A well-structured content calendar includes deadlines, publication dates, and promotional activities.

6. Distribution and Promotion

Creating great content is only half the battle; effective distribution and promotion are equally important. Businesses should leverage multiple channels, such as social media, email marketing, and search engine optimization (SEO), to amplify their content's reach. Collaborating with influencers and partners can also extend the content's visibility to a broader audience.

7. Measure and Analyze Performance

To gauge the effectiveness of the content strategy, it's essential to track key performance indicators (KPIs) such as website traffic, engagement metrics, lead generation, and conversion rates. Analyzing these metrics provides insights into what works and what needs improvement, enabling businesses to refine their strategy over time.

Types of Content and Their Roles

A robust content marketing strategy employs a variety of content types, each serving a unique role in engaging and converting the audience. The following sections explore some of the most common types of content and their significance.

1. Blogs

Blogs are a cornerstone of content marketing. They offer a platform for sharing in-depth articles, industry insights, how-to guides, and thought leadership pieces (content created by experts or leaders in a particular field). Blogging helps drive organic traffic by improving search engine rankings through keyword optimization and valuable content. Additionally, blogs establish the brand's expertise and provide a resource hub for the audience, fostering trust and loyalty.

2. Videos

Video content has surged in popularity due to its engaging and easily consumable nature. Videos can take various forms, including explainer videos, product demonstrations, customer testimonials, and behind-the-scenes glimpses. They are highly effective in conveying complex information, evoking emotions, and enhancing brand storytelling. *Brand storytelling* is the practice of using narrative techniques to create a compelling and relatable story about a brand, its values, and its products or services, aiming to connect emotionally with the audience and build a strong, lasting relationship. With platforms like YouTube and social media favoring video content, incorporating videos into the content strategy can significantly boost audience engagement and reach.

3. Infographics

Infographics are visual representations of information, data, or knowledge designed to present complex information quickly and clearly, using elements like charts, graphs, icons, and text to enhance understanding and retention. Infographics combine visuals and concise text to present information in a visually appealing and easily digestible format. They are particularly useful for simplifying complex data, illustrating processes, and presenting statistics. Infographics are highly shareable, making them ideal for increasing brand visibility and driving traffic from social media and other online platforms.

4. E-books and Whitepapers

E-books and whitepapers are long-form content pieces that provide in-depth insights into specific topics. They are valuable for showcasing expertise, educating the audience, and generating leads. By offering these resources in exchange for contact information, businesses can build their email lists and nurture leads through targeted email marketing campaigns.

5. Case Studies

Case studies highlight real-life examples of how a product or service has benefited a customer. They provide tangible proof of the brand's value and effectiveness, making them powerful tools for building credibility and trust. Case studies are particularly effective in the consideration stage of the buyer's journey, helping prospects make informed decisions.

6. Social Media Posts

Social media platforms offer diverse opportunities for content marketing. Short-form posts, including text, images, and videos, enable businesses to engage with their audience in real-time. Social media content can range from promotional updates and user-generated content to interactive polls and live streams. Leveraging social media effectively requires understanding the unique characteristics and audience preferences of each platform.

7. Podcasts

Podcasts have gained traction as an alternative form of content consumption. They allow businesses to share valuable insights, interviews, and stories in an audio format that audiences can enjoy on the go. Podcasts are excellent for building a loyal following and establishing a brand's voice and personality.

8. Webinars

Webinars are live or recorded online presentations that provide educational content, demonstrations, or discussions. They offer an interactive platform for engaging with the audience, answering questions, and showcasing expertise. Webinars are particularly effective for lead generation and nurturing, as they provide valuable information in exchange for attendee registration.

Integrating Content Marketing with Other Digital Strategies

To maximize the impact of content marketing, it should be integrated with other digital marketing strategies. SEO plays a crucial role in ensuring that content is discoverable by search engines and reaches the target audience. By optimizing content with relevant keywords, meta tags, and backlinks, businesses can improve their search engine rankings and drive organic traffic.

Social media marketing complements content marketing by providing platforms for content distribution and engagement. Sharing content on social media amplifies its reach and encourages audience interaction. Paid advertising on social media can further enhance content visibility and target specific demographics.

Email marketing is another powerful tool for distributing content and nurturing leads. By segmenting email lists and delivering personalized content, businesses can keep their audience engaged and drive conversions. Email newsletters, drip campaigns, and automated workflows can be used to share blog posts, e-books, and other valuable content.

Conclusion

Content marketing is an essential pillar of modern digital marketing strategies. By creating valuable and relevant content, businesses can attract and engage their target audience, build trust and credibility, and drive meaningful results. Developing a content strategy involves understanding the audience, planning diverse content types, and leveraging multiple distribution channels. As the digital landscape continues to evolve, businesses that prioritize content marketing will be better positioned to connect with their audience and achieve their marketing objectives.

Chapter 10. Blogging for Business Success

Introduction

In today's digital age, blogging has become an indispensable tool for businesses looking to establish a strong online presence. It offers a dynamic platform to share knowledge, engage with audiences, and drive traffic to websites. A well-executed blog can boost search engine rankings, enhance brand visibility, and ultimately, contribute to business success. This chapter delves into effective blogging strategies for engagement and SEO, and explores the role of AI in enhancing content creation.

The Importance of Blogging in Digital Marketing

Blogging serves as a cornerstone of digital marketing, offering a multifaceted approach to communication and engagement. For businesses, a blog is not just a medium to disseminate information but a powerful tool to build relationships, foster trust, and convert readers into customers. By consistently providing valuable content, businesses can position themselves as industry leaders, addressing customer pain points and offering solutions.

Effective Blogging Strategies for Engagement

Creating engaging content is paramount to the success of a business blog. Engagement refers to the level of interaction that readers have with your content, including comments, shares, and likes. Here are several strategies to enhance blog engagement.

1. Know Your Audience: Understanding your target audience is the first step in creating content that resonates.

Conduct market research to identify the demographics, preferences, and pain points of your readers. Tailor your content to address their needs and interests.

2. **Compelling Headlines:** The headline is the first thing a reader sees, and it needs to be captivating enough to draw them in. Use strong, action-oriented words, and consider using numbers or questions to pique curiosity.

3. **Quality Over Quantity:** While frequent posting is important, quality should never be compromised. Each blog post should offer unique insights, actionable advice, or valuable information that readers can't easily find elsewhere.

4. **Visual Content:** Incorporate images, infographics, and videos to make your posts more visually appealing. Visual content breaks up the text and can make complex information more digestible.

5. **Encourage Interaction:** Prompt readers to engage with your content by asking questions, encouraging comments, and responding to feedback. Interactive content such as quizzes and polls can also drive engagement.

6. **Share Personal Stories:** Authenticity resonates with readers. Sharing personal anecdotes and experiences can create a deeper connection and make your content more relatable.

SEO Strategies for Blogging

Search engine optimization (SEO) is crucial for ensuring that your blog reaches a wider audience. By optimizing your content for search engines, you can improve your visibility and attract organic traffic. Here are some effective SEO strategies for blogging.

1. Keyword Research: **Identify relevant keywords that your target audience is searching for.** Use tools like Google Keyword Planner, SEMrush, or Ahrefs to find keywords with high search volume and low competition. Incorporate these keywords naturally into your content, including in headlines, subheadings, and body text.

2. On-Page SEO: **Optimize each blog post by using keywords in the title, meta descriptions, and URL.** Ensure that your blog is structured with proper headings (H1, H2, H3) to improve readability and SEO.

3. Quality Backlinks: **Build backlinks from reputable websites to enhance your blog's authority.** Guest posting, collaborating with influencers, and participating in industry forums are effective ways to gain quality backlinks.

4. Internal Linking: **Link to other relevant posts within your blog to keep readers on your site longer and improve SEO.** Internal links also help search engines understand the structure of your site.

5. Mobile Optimization: **Ensure that your blog is mobile-friendly.** With the increasing use of mobile devices, search engines prioritize mobile-optimized content in their rankings.

6. Page Load Speed: **A slow-loading page can deter readers and negatively impact your SEO.** Optimize images, use caching plugins, and choose a reliable hosting provider to improve page load speed.

Using AI to Enhance Content Creation

Artificial intelligence (AI) is revolutionizing content creation by offering tools and technologies that enhance efficiency and creativity. Here are some ways AI can be leveraged to improve your blogging efforts.

1. Content Ideation: AI-powered tools like HubSpot's Blog Ideas Generator or BuzzSumo can help generate content ideas based on trending topics and audience interests. These tools analyze vast amounts of data to suggest relevant and engaging topics.

2. Writing Assistance: AI writing assistants like Grammarly, Hemingway, and Jasper (formerly Jarvis) can help improve the quality of your writing. They provide real-time suggestions for grammar, style, and readability, ensuring that your content is polished and professional.

3. SEO Optimization: AI tools like Clearscope and MarketMuse analyze your content and provide recommendations to improve SEO. They suggest keywords, related terms, and content structures that can enhance your search engine rankings.

4. Personalization: AI can analyze user behavior and preferences to deliver personalized content recommendations. This tailored approach can increase engagement and make your readers feel valued.

5. Automated Content Creation: Advanced AI tools can generate content automatically based on specific parameters. For instance, tools like Copy.ai and Writesonic can create product descriptions, social media posts, and even full-length articles. While human oversight is still

necessary, these tools can save time and streamline the content creation process.

6. Analytics and Insights: AI-powered analytics tools like Google Analytics and SEMrush offer insights into how your content is performing. They track metrics such as page views, bounce rates, and user engagement, helping you refine your content strategy for better results.

Conclusion

Blogging is a powerful component of digital marketing that can drive business success when executed effectively. By creating engaging content and implementing robust SEO strategies, businesses can enhance their online presence and attract a loyal audience. The integration of AI in content creation further amplifies these efforts, offering innovative solutions to streamline processes and improve quality.

In summary, the key to successful business blogging lies in understanding your audience, delivering valuable content, and optimizing for search engines. Embrace the advancements in AI to stay ahead in the competitive digital landscape. As you continue to refine your blogging strategy, remember that consistency, authenticity, and a focus on the reader's needs are the pillars that will support your journey to success.

Blogging for business is not a one-size-fits-all approach. It requires continuous learning, adaptation, and a willingness to experiment with new techniques. Stay abreast of the latest trends in digital marketing and AI to ensure that your blog remains relevant and effective. With dedication and the right strategies, your business blog can become a cornerstone of your digital marketing success, driving engagement, growth, and profitability.

Chapter 11. Social Media Marketing

Introduction

Social media marketing has transformed the way businesses engage with their audience, promote their products, and cultivate their brand presence. It is an integral component of digital marketing, leveraging various platforms to reach, engage, and convert potential customers. This article delves into the strategies for different social media platforms, explores how to measure and analyze social media ROI, and provides insights into creating effective campaigns.

Understanding Social Media Marketing

Social media marketing involves using social media platforms to connect with an audience to build a brand, increase sales, and drive website traffic. This involves publishing great content on social media profiles, listening to and engaging followers, analyzing results, and running social media advertisements. Major social media platforms include Facebook, Instagram, X (Twitter), LinkedIn, Pinterest, YouTube, and Snapchat. Each platform requires a tailored approach to maximize effectiveness.

Strategies for Different Platforms

1. Facebook

Facebook is the largest social media platform, making it a cornerstone for any social media marketing strategy. Its diverse user base allows businesses to target a broad audience. Effective Facebook marketing strategies include:

Content Variety: Posting a mix of content types such as videos, images, links, and text updates keeps the audience engaged. Video content, especially live videos, tend to receive higher engagement.

Targeted Advertising: Facebook Ads allows businesses to target users based on demographics, interests, and behaviors. Utilizing Facebook's ad targeting capabilities can enhance the reach and effectiveness of marketing campaigns.

Community Building: Creating and nurturing a Facebook group related to your niche can foster a sense of community. Engaging with group members and providing value through exclusive content can build brand loyalty.

Analytics Utilization: Facebook Insights provides valuable data on post engagement, reach, and audience demographics, helping businesses refine their strategies.

2. Instagram

Instagram, known for its visual-centric approach, is ideal for brands focusing on imagery and short videos. Key strategies include:

Aesthetic Consistency: Maintaining a consistent visual style that aligns with your brand identity helps in creating a recognizable and appealing feed.

Utilizing Stories and Reels: Instagram Stories and Reels are excellent tools for showcasing behind-the-scenes content, promotions, and user-generated content, keeping the audience engaged with fresh and dynamic content.

Influencer Collaborations: **Partnering with influencers who resonate with your brand can extend your reach and credibility. Influencers can introduce your products to their dedicated followers in an authentic manner.**

Hashtags and Location Tags: **Using relevant hashtags and location tags increases the discoverability of posts, attracting users who are searching for specific content.**

3. LinkedIn

LinkedIn is the premier platform for B2B marketing, professional networking, and industry thought leadership. *B2B marketing*, or business-to-business marketing, refers to the strategies and practices used by companies to promote their products or services to other businesses, rather than to individual consumers. This type of marketing focuses on building relationships, addressing business needs, and emphasizing the value and benefits of the offering in a professional context. Effective strategies include:

Thought Leadership Content: **Publishing articles and posts that showcase your expertise in your industry can position your brand as a thought leader. Sharing insights, trends, and case studies can attract a professional audience.**

Engaging Company Page: **An active and engaging company page with regular updates, job postings, and industry news can attract followers and potential clients.**

LinkedIn Ads: **Sponsored content, InMail, and dynamic ads on LinkedIn allow for precise targeting based on job title, company size, industry, and more, making it an effective tool for B2B campaigns.**

Employee Advocacy: Encouraging employees to share company content and their professional experiences can broaden your brand's reach and build trust.

4. X (Twitter)

X (Twitter) is a platform for real-time updates and customer engagement. Key strategies include:

Timely Engagement: Responding promptly to mentions, comments, and direct messages enhances customer satisfaction and shows that your brand values its audience.

Trending Hashtags: Participating in trending conversations by using relevant hashtags can increase visibility and engagement. However, ensure that the trends are relevant to your brand.

Short, Impactful Content: Crafting concise and impactful tweets with a clear message or call-to-action is crucial, given Twitter's character limit.

X (Twitter) Chats: Hosting or participating in X (Twitter) chats on industry-related topics can increase brand visibility and foster community engagement.

5. YouTube

YouTube is the go-to platform for video content, offering immense potential for educational and promotional videos. Effective strategies include:

High-Quality Content: Producing high-quality videos that provide value, such as tutorials, product demos, and customer testimonials, can attract and retain viewers.

SEO for Videos: Optimizing video titles, descriptions, and tags with relevant keywords can enhance discoverability on YouTube and search engines.

Consistent Upload Schedule: Regularly uploading videos on a consistent schedule keeps your audience engaged and coming back for more content.

Engagement with Viewers: Responding to comments, asking for feedback, and encouraging viewers to like, share, and subscribe fosters a loyal community.

Measuring and Analyzing Social Media ROI

Measuring the return on investment (ROI) from social media marketing is crucial for understanding the effectiveness of your strategies and justifying your marketing spend. Here's how to measure and analyze social media ROI.

1. Setting Clear Goals

The first step in measuring ROI is setting clear, measurable goals. These goals could include increasing brand awareness, generating leads, driving website traffic, or boosting sales. Each goal should have specific metrics associated with it, such as follower growth, engagement rate, conversion rate, or revenue generated.

2. Tracking Key Metrics

Different platforms offer various metrics that can be tracked to measure performance. Common metrics include:

Reach and Impressions: These metrics indicate how many people have seen your content and how often. They are essential for measuring brand awareness.

Engagement: Likes, comments, shares, and clicks are indicators of how well your audience is interacting with your content. High engagement rates often correlate with effective content.

Conversion Rate: This metric measures how many users take a desired action after engaging with your social media content, such as filling out a form or making a purchase.

Click-Through Rate (CTR): CTR indicates the effectiveness of your call-to-actions and how compelling your content is in driving traffic to your website or landing pages.

Customer Acquisition Cost (CAC): This measures the cost associated with acquiring a new customer through social media marketing efforts.

3. Using Analytics Tools

Platforms like Facebook, Instagram, and LinkedIn offer built-in analytics tools that provide detailed insights into performance metrics. Additionally, tools like Google Analytics can track social media traffic to your website, providing a comprehensive view of how social media efforts translate into web activity and conversions.

4. Calculating ROI

To calculate social media ROI, use the following formula:

ROI = (Net Profit / Total Investment) * 100

Net profit can be calculated by subtracting the total investment in social media marketing (including ad spend, content creation costs, and labor) from the revenue generated through social media efforts.

5. A/B Testing

A/B testing involves creating two versions of a social media post or ad and comparing their performance to determine which one is more effective. This helps in optimizing content and improving ROI by focusing on what resonates best with the audience.

6. Reporting and Analysis

Regularly reviewing and analyzing performance reports is crucial for understanding what works and what doesn't. This analysis should inform future strategies, helping to refine content, targeting, and overall approach to maximize ROI.

Conclusion

Social media marketing is a dynamic and multifaceted component of digital marketing that requires a strategic approach tailored to each platform. By understanding the unique characteristics and audiences of platforms like Facebook, Instagram, LinkedIn, X (Twitter), and YouTube, businesses can create effective marketing strategies that engage and convert their target audience. Measuring and analyzing social media ROI is essential for assessing the effectiveness of these strategies and making informed decisions to optimize performance. With the right approach, social media marketing can significantly contribute to brand growth, customer engagement, and business success.

Chapter 12. Brand Design and Digital Presence

Introduction

In today's digital age, where the online marketplace is bustling with competition, the importance of a strong brand identity and digital presence cannot be overstated. A comprehensive understanding of brand design and its influence on digital platforms is crucial for businesses aiming to establish a significant footprint in the virtual world. This chapter delves into the nuances of creating a robust brand identity and the design principles that should guide businesses in crafting their digital presence.

Creating a Strong Brand Identity Online

1. Understanding Brand Identity

Brand identity is the collection of all elements that a company creates to portray the right image to its consumer. This encompasses everything from the logo and color scheme to the tone of voice used in communications. In the digital realm, brand identity is even more critical as it represents the business in a space where personal interaction is minimal. A well-crafted brand identity can differentiate a company from its competitors, build customer loyalty, and foster trust.

2. Elements of Brand Identity

Logo and Visual Elements: The logo is often the first thing customers associate with a brand. It should be unique, memorable, and reflective of the brand's values and mission. Alongside the logo, visual elements such as color schemes, typography, and imagery play a crucial role. These elements should be consistent across all digital platforms to ensure a cohesive brand presence.

Brand Voice and Messaging: How a brand communicates with its audience can significantly impact its perception. The brand voice should be consistent and align with the brand's personality. Whether it's through social media posts, website content, or email newsletters, the messaging should resonate with the target audience and reflect the brand's core values.

User Experience (UX): A strong brand identity also translates into an excellent user experience. A well-designed website or app that is easy to navigate and visually appealing can leave a lasting impression on users. Consistency in design and functionality across various digital touchpoints reinforces the brand identity and ensures a seamless user experience.

Strategies for Building a Strong Brand Identity Online

1. Research and Understanding the Audience: Knowing the target audience is the foundation of building a strong brand identity. Businesses should invest time in understanding their audience's needs, preferences, and behaviors. This insight helps in tailoring the brand's visual and verbal elements to resonate with the audience effectively.

2. Consistency is Key: Consistency in brand identity across all digital platforms is crucial. This includes maintaining uniformity in visual elements, messaging, and user experience. Consistent branding helps in building recognition and trust among the audience.

3. Engagement and Interaction: Active engagement with the audience through social media, blogs, and other digital platforms can strengthen brand identity. Responding to comments, participating in discussions, and creating interactive content can make the brand more relatable and trustworthy.

4. Adaptability and Evolution: While consistency is important, brands should also be adaptable and open to evolution. The digital landscape is dynamic, and staying relevant requires periodic updates to the brand identity. This could be in response to changes in consumer preferences, technological advancements, or market trends.

Design Principles for Digital Platforms

1. User-Centric Design

User-centric design is a fundamental principle for digital platforms. It focuses on creating a positive user experience by prioritizing the needs and preferences of the users. This involves understanding user behavior, designing intuitive interfaces, and ensuring that the digital platform is accessible and easy to use.

Simplicity and Clarity: Digital designs should be simple and clear. Overly complex designs can confuse users and detract from the user experience. Clear navigation, minimalistic layouts, and straightforward content presentation can enhance usability.

Responsiveness and Accessibility: With the increasing use of mobile devices, ensuring that digital platforms are responsive is essential. Responsive design ensures that the platform works well on various devices and screen sizes. Additionally, accessibility considerations, such as alt text for images and keyboard navigation, make the platform usable for all users, including those with disabilities.

2. Visual Hierarchy and Layout

Visual hierarchy and layout play a significant role in guiding users through digital content. By strategically arranging elements on the page, designers can direct users' attention to the most important information.

Contrast and Emphasis: Using contrast effectively can highlight key elements such as calls to action (CTAs), headlines, and important messages. Emphasis can be achieved through variations in size, color, and placement.

Consistent Layouts: Consistent layouts across different pages of a website or sections of an app help users predict where to find information, thereby enhancing their experience. Grid systems and modular designs are effective techniques for maintaining consistency.

3. Color Theory and Typography

Color and typography are powerful tools in digital design. They not only enhance the aesthetic appeal but also influence user emotions and behavior.

Color Psychology: Different colors evoke different emotions. For instance, blue is often associated with trust and calm, while red can signify urgency or excitement. Understanding color psychology can help in selecting a color scheme that aligns with the brand's identity and evokes the desired response from users.

Readable Typography: Typography should be readable and align with the brand's personality. Choosing the right font size, style, and spacing can make a significant difference in how users perceive and interact with the content. A combination of serif and sans-serif fonts, along with appropriate heading hierarchies, can enhance readability and visual appeal.

4. Interactive and Dynamic Elements

Incorporating interactive and dynamic elements can enhance user engagement and create a more immersive experience. These elements can include animations, micro-interactions, and multimedia content.

Animations and Micro-Interactions: **Subtle animations and micro-interactions can make the digital experience more engaging. These can include hover effects, button animations, and loading indicators, which provide feedback to users and make the interface feel more responsive.**

Multimedia Content: **Videos, infographics, and interactive graphics can make content more engaging and easier to understand. However, it's important to ensure that multimedia content does not slow down the platform or compromise the user experience.**

5. Performance and Speed

Performance and speed are critical factors in digital design. Slow-loading websites or apps can frustrate users and lead to high bounce rates.

Optimizing Load Times: **Optimizing images, using efficient coding practices, and leveraging content delivery networks (CDNs) can improve load times. Content Delivery Networks are systems of distributed servers that deliver web content to users based on their geographic** location to improve access speed and reliability. Faster platforms provide a better user experience and can positively impact search engine rankings.

Testing and Iteration: Regular testing and iteration are essential to maintain optimal performance. This involves conducting usability tests, monitoring performance metrics, and making necessary adjustments to improve speed and functionality.

Conclusion

In the realm of digital marketing, a strong brand identity and effective digital design are paramount. They not only differentiate a brand from its competitors but also foster trust and loyalty among consumers. By understanding the elements that constitute a strong brand identity and adhering to user-centric design principles, businesses can create compelling digital experiences that resonate with their audience.

The journey to establishing a robust digital presence is ongoing, requiring constant adaptation and evolution. As technology advances and consumer preferences shift, brands must remain agile and willing to refine their digital strategies. Ultimately, the fusion of a well-defined brand identity and meticulous digital design can propel a business to new heights in the digital landscape, driving engagement, loyalty, and success.

Chapter 13. Effective Product Marketing in the Digital Landscape

Introduction

In the rapidly evolving digital age, marketing strategies must adapt to the changing landscape to remain effective. Product marketing, a critical component of any business strategy, requires an innovative approach when dealing with online platforms. This article delves into the various strategies and tools necessary for launching and promoting products online, offering a comprehensive guide to navigating the digital marketplace.

Understanding the Digital Landscape

The digital landscape is vast and continuously expanding, characterized by an array of platforms, channels, and tools that connect businesses with their target audiences. To effectively market products in this environment, one must first understand the intricacies of the digital ecosystem. This includes social media platforms, search engines, email marketing, content marketing, and e-commerce sites, among others. Each platform offers unique opportunities and challenges, requiring tailored strategies to maximize their potential.

Strategies for Launching Products Online

Launching a product in the digital world requires meticulous planning and execution. Here are key strategies to consider.

1. Market Research and Analysis

Before launching a product, thorough market research is essential. Understanding the target audience, their preferences, and pain points helps in tailoring the product and marketing messages. Utilize tools like Google Analytics, social media insights, and surveys to gather data. Analyze competitors to identify gaps in the market and potential opportunities.

2. Creating a Buzz Pre-Launch

Generating excitement before the official launch is crucial. Use teasers and sneak peeks to create anticipation. Social media platforms like Instagram, Twitter, and Facebook are ideal for this purpose. Engage with potential customers through interactive content such as polls, contests, and countdowns. Collaborate with influencers and bloggers who can amplify your message to a broader audience.

3. Building a Landing Page

A landing page is a standalone web page designed specifically for marketing or advertising campaigns to capture visitor information or prompt a specific action. A dedicated landing page is an effective tool for capturing leads and providing detailed information about the upcoming product. Ensure the landing page is visually appealing, with clear calls-to-action (CTAs) for pre-orders or newsletter sign-ups. Use this page to collect email addresses, which can be used for targeted email marketing campaigns.

4. Leveraging Email Marketing

Email marketing remains a powerful tool for product launches. Create a series of automated emails to nurture leads collected from the landing page. These emails should build anticipation, provide valuable information, and encourage pre-orders or sign-ups. Personalize emails to enhance engagement and make potential customers feel valued.

5. Utilizing Social Media Marketing

Social media platforms offer unparalleled reach and engagement. Develop a comprehensive social media strategy that includes organic posts, paid advertisements, and influencer collaborations. Use engaging visuals, videos, and stories to capture the audience's attention. Monitor engagement metrics and adjust the strategy as needed to optimize results.

6. Influencer and Affiliate Marketing

Influencers are individuals with a significant online following who promote products or services to their audience, while affiliates are partners who earn a commission by promoting and driving sales for a company's products or services. Influencers and affiliates can significantly boost the visibility of a new product. Identify influencers whose audience aligns with your target market and collaborate on promotional content. Affiliate marketing, where partners earn a commission for driving sales, can also expand your reach. Provide affiliates with the necessary resources and incentives to promote your product effectively.

Promoting Products Online

Once the product is launched, sustained promotion is necessary to maintain momentum and drive sales. Here are some effective strategies.

1. Search Engine Optimization (SEO)

SEO is critical for improving the visibility of your product in search engine results. Optimize your website and product pages with relevant keywords, high-quality content, and backlinks. Ensure that the website is mobile-friendly and has fast loading times, as these factors influence search engine rankings. Regularly update content to keep it fresh and relevant.

2. Pay-Per-Click (PPC) Advertising

PPC advertising, such as Google Ads, allows you to target specific keywords and demographics. This method provides immediate visibility and can drive significant traffic to your product pages. Carefully plan and manage PPC campaigns to ensure a good return on investment (ROI). Use A/B testing to optimize ad creatives and landing pages for better performance.

3. Content Marketing

Content marketing involves creating and distributing valuable, relevant content to attract and engage your target audience. Develop a content strategy that includes blog posts, videos, infographics, and e-books related to your product. Share this content across various channels to drive traffic and build brand authority. Guest blogging and collaborations with industry experts can further extend your reach.

4. Social Media Advertising

Paid social media campaigns can enhance your reach and engagement. Platforms like Facebook, Instagram, and LinkedIn offer advanced targeting options, allowing you to reach specific demographics and interests. Experiment with different ad formats, such as carousel ads, video ads, and sponsored posts, to determine what resonates best with your audience. *Carousel ads* are interactive advertisements that allow users to swipe through multiple images or videos within a single ad unit, often used to showcase a variety of products or features.

5. Retargeting Campaigns

Retargeting campaigns target users who have previously interacted with your website or ads but did not make a purchase. Use retargeting ads to remind these users about your product and encourage them to complete their purchase. This strategy helps in converting warm leads into customers by keeping your product top-of-mind.

6. Leveraging User-Generated Content

User-generated content (UGC), such as reviews, testimonials, and social media posts from customers, can be a powerful promotional tool. Encourage satisfied customers to share their experiences and feature their content on your platforms. UGC adds authenticity and trust to your brand, influencing potential customers' purchasing decisions.

Utilizing Digital Tools for Market Penetration

To effectively penetrate the market, leveraging digital tools is essential. These tools can help streamline processes, enhance efficiency, and provide valuable insights. Here are some key tools to consider.

1. Customer Relationship Management (CRM) Systems

CRM (Customer Relationship Management) systems are software platforms that help businesses manage, track, and analyze customer interactions and data throughout the customer lifecycle to improve relationships and drive sales growth. CRM systems like Salesforce, HubSpot, and Zoho help manage customer interactions, track leads, and nurture relationships. These systems provide valuable insights into customer behavior, enabling personalized marketing efforts. Use CRM data to segment your audience and tailor marketing campaigns to specific customer needs.

2. Marketing Automation Platforms

Marketing Automation Platforms are software solutions designed to automate marketing tasks and workflows, streamline marketing processes, and measure the effectiveness of marketing campaigns across multiple channels. Marketing automation platforms, such as Marketo and Mailchimp, allow you to automate repetitive tasks like email marketing, social media posting, and ad campaigns. Automation enhances efficiency and ensures consistent communication with your audience. Use these platforms to create personalized, data-driven marketing workflows that nurture leads and drive conversions.

3. Analytics and Reporting Tools

Tools like Google Analytics, SEMrush, and Ahrefs provide detailed insights into website traffic, user behavior, and campaign performance. Use these tools to monitor key metrics, identify trends, and make data-driven decisions.

Regularly review and analyze data to optimize marketing strategies and achieve better results.

4. Social Media Management Tools

Social Media Management involves the process of creating, scheduling, analyzing, and engaging with content posted on social media platforms to build and maintain a brand's online presence and community. Managing multiple social media accounts can be challenging. Tools like Hootsuite, Buffer, and Sprout Social simplify this process by allowing you to schedule posts, monitor engagement, and analyze performance across platforms. These tools help maintain a consistent social media presence and improve audience engagement.

5. E-commerce Platforms

E-commerce Platforms are online software solutions that enable businesses to create, manage, and operate digital storefronts for selling products and services directly to consumers over the internet. If you are selling products online, choosing the right e-commerce platform is crucial. Platforms like Shopify, WooCommerce, and BigCommerce offer robust features for managing product listings, processing payments, and tracking orders. Ensure that your e-commerce platform integrates seamlessly with other marketing tools to provide a cohesive user experience.

Measuring Success and Adapting Strategies

Effective product marketing in the digital landscape requires continuous measurement and adaptation. Set clear goals and key performance indicators (KPIs) for your marketing efforts. Regularly review performance data and adjust strategies as needed to achieve your objectives. Stay updated with industry trends and emerging technologies to stay ahead of the competition.

Conclusion

The digital landscape offers immense opportunities for product marketing, but it also presents unique challenges. By understanding the digital ecosystem, employing strategic planning, leveraging digital tools, and continuously measuring and adapting your efforts, you can effectively launch and promote products online. This comprehensive approach ensures that your marketing efforts are not only effective but also sustainable in the ever-evolving digital world.

Chapter 14. Digital Marketing Campaigns Planning and Execution

Introduction

In the rapidly evolving landscape of digital marketing, the ability to plan and execute effective campaigns is crucial for businesses seeking to engage their audience, build brand awareness, and drive conversions. A well-orchestrated digital marketing campaign requires a strategic approach, encompassing a clear understanding of the target audience, meticulous planning, and the use of various digital tools and techniques to monitor and optimize performance. This chapter delves into the comprehensive steps necessary for creating successful digital marketing campaigns, along with the tools and techniques for monitoring and optimizing these campaigns.

Understanding the Fundamentals of Digital Marketing Campaigns

Before diving into the intricacies of planning and execution, it is essential to grasp the fundamental principles of digital marketing campaigns. A digital marketing campaign is a coordinated set of online marketing activities designed to achieve specific business objectives. These objectives can range from increasing brand awareness and generating leads to driving sales and fostering customer loyalty. The success of a digital marketing campaign hinges on a clear understanding of the target audience, a well-defined strategy, and the effective use of various digital channels and platforms.

Steps for Creating Successful Digital Marketing Campaigns

1. Define Clear Objectives

The foundation of any successful digital marketing campaign lies in defining clear, measurable objectives. These objectives should align with the overall business goals and provide a clear direction for the campaign. Common objectives include increasing website traffic, generating leads, boosting social media engagement, and driving sales. Setting SMART (Specific, Measurable, Achievable, Relevant, Time-bound) goals is essential to ensure that the campaign's progress can be tracked and evaluated effectively.

2. Understand the Target Audience

A deep understanding of the target audience is crucial for crafting messages and selecting channels that resonate with potential customers. Conduct thorough market research to identify the demographics, interests, behaviors, and pain points of your target audience. Creating detailed buyer personas can help in visualizing and segmenting the audience, enabling more personalized and effective marketing efforts.

3. Develop a Comprehensive Strategy

With clear objectives and a thorough understanding of the target audience, the next step is to develop a comprehensive strategy. This strategy should outline the key messages, content themes, and digital channels to be used. Consider the strengths and weaknesses of various channels such as social media, email marketing, search engine marketing, and content marketing. A well-rounded strategy often involves a mix of these channels to maximize reach and impact.

4. Create Compelling Content

Content is the cornerstone of any digital marketing campaign. High-quality, engaging content can capture the audience's attention, convey key messages, and drive desired actions. Develop a content plan that aligns with the campaign objectives and resonates with the target audience. This plan should include a mix of content types such as blog posts, videos, infographics, social media posts, and email newsletters. Ensure that the content is optimized for search engines (SEO) to enhance visibility and reach.

5. Implement and Execute

With the strategy and content in place, it is time to implement and execute the campaign. This involves publishing content, launching ads, and engaging with the audience across various digital channels. Use scheduling tools to plan and automate social media posts and email campaigns. Monitor the initial response and make necessary adjustments to optimize performance. Consistent execution is key to maintaining momentum and achieving the desired outcomes.

Tools and Techniques for Monitoring and Optimizing Campaigns

1. Analytics and Reporting Tools

Monitoring the performance of a digital marketing campaign requires robust analytics and reporting tools. Google Analytics is a powerful tool that provides insights into website traffic, user behavior, and conversion rates. It allows marketers to track the effectiveness of different channels and identify areas for improvement. Social media platforms like Facebook, X (Twitter), and LinkedIn also offer built-in analytics tools to measure engagement and reach. Regularly reviewing these metrics helps in understanding what is working and what needs adjustment.

2. A/B Testing

A/B testing, or split testing, is a technique used to compare two versions of a webpage, email, or ad to determine which one performs better. By testing different headlines, images, calls to action, and other elements, marketers can identify the most effective combinations and optimize their campaigns accordingly. Tools like Optimizely, Unbounce, and Google Optimize facilitate A/B testing and provide actionable insights to enhance campaign performance.

3. SEO Tools

Search engine optimization (SEO) is a critical component of digital marketing. Tools like Ahrefs, SEMrush, and Moz help in conducting keyword research, analyzing competitors, and tracking search rankings. These tools provide valuable data on search volume, keyword difficulty, and backlink profiles, enabling marketers to optimize their content for better visibility on search engines. Regular SEO audits ensure that the website remains optimized and continues to attract organic traffic.

4. Social Media Management Tools

Managing multiple social media accounts can be challenging without the right tools. Social media management platforms like Hootsuite, Buffer, and Sprout Social allow marketers to schedule posts, monitor mentions, and engage with followers from a single dashboard. These tools also provide analytics to measure the performance of social media campaigns and identify trends. Effective social media management ensures consistent brand presence and timely responses to audience interactions.

5. Email Marketing Platforms

Email marketing remains a powerful tool for nurturing leads and driving conversions. Platforms like Mailchimp, Constant Contact, and HubSpot offer features such as email templates, automation workflows, and segmentation capabilities. These platforms enable marketers to send personalized and targeted emails based on user behavior and preferences. Monitoring metrics like open rates, click-through rates, and conversion rates helps in refining email campaigns and improving their effectiveness.

6. Conversion Rate Optimization (CRO) Tools

Conversion rate optimization (CRO) focuses on improving the percentage of website visitors who take desired actions, such as making a purchase or filling out a form. Tools like Crazy Egg, Hotjar, and VWO provide insights into user behavior through heatmaps, session recordings, and user feedback. *Heatmaps* are graphical representations of data where individual values are represented by varying colors to show patterns and variations. By analyzing how users interact with the website, marketers can identify obstacles and make data-driven changes to enhance the user experience and increase conversions.

7. Paid Advertising Platforms

Paid advertising is an essential component of many digital marketing campaigns. Platforms like Google Ads, Facebook Ads, and LinkedIn Ads allow marketers to create targeted ad campaigns and reach specific audiences. These platforms offer detailed targeting options based on demographics, interests, and behaviors. Monitoring the performance of paid ads through metrics like click-through rates, conversion rates, and return on ad spend (ROAS) helps in optimizing ad campaigns for better results.

Continuous Optimization and Improvement

A successful digital marketing campaign is not a one-time effort but an ongoing process of optimization and improvement. Regularly reviewing performance metrics, analyzing data, and staying updated with industry trends are crucial for maintaining and enhancing campaign effectiveness. Conduct periodic audits to identify strengths, weaknesses, and opportunities for improvement. Stay agile and be willing to experiment with new strategies and tactics to keep the campaign fresh and relevant.

Conclusion

Planning and executing successful digital marketing campaigns require a strategic approach, a deep understanding of the target audience, and the effective use of various tools and techniques. By defining clear objectives, developing a comprehensive strategy, creating compelling content, and leveraging analytics and optimization tools, businesses can maximize the impact of their digital marketing efforts. Continuous monitoring and improvement ensure that campaigns remain effective and deliver the desired results. As the digital landscape continues to evolve, staying adaptable and innovative will be key to sustained success in digital marketing.

Chapter 15. Email Marketing

Introduction

Email marketing stands as one of the most powerful tools in the digital marketer's arsenal. Despite the proliferation of social media and other communication channels, email remains a direct, personal, and highly effective means of reaching and engaging with an audience. This chapter explores the intricacies of email marketing, offering insights into building and segmenting email lists, crafting compelling campaigns, and maximizing the impact of this versatile medium.

Building and Segmenting Email Lists

The foundation of any successful email marketing strategy is a robust and well-segmented email list. The quality of your email list determines the effectiveness of your campaigns. Building this list starts with a clear understanding of your target audience and the value you can provide them.

List Building Techniques

One of the most common methods of building an email list is through opt-in forms on your website. These forms should be strategically placed in high-traffic areas such as the homepage, blog posts, and landing pages. Offering valuable content, like ebooks, whitepapers, or exclusive discounts, in exchange for email addresses can significantly boost your sign-up rate. It's essential to ensure that your opt-in process is straightforward and respects privacy concerns, adhering to regulations like GDPR and CAN-SPAM Act.

GDPR (General Data Protection Regulation): A regulation in EU law on data protection and privacy for all individuals within the European Union and the European Economic Area, emphasizing individual rights over personal data and data protection.

CAN-SPAM Act (Controlling the Assault of Non-Solicited Pornography And Marketing): A U.S. law establishing rules for commercial emails, giving recipients the right to have businesses stop emailing them, and outlining penalties for violations.

Another effective technique is leveraging social media platforms. Promoting your email sign-up form on social media can attract your followers to join your mailing list. Additionally, hosting webinars, online events, or running contests and giveaways can also be excellent ways to collect email addresses.

Segmentation Strategies

Segmentation involves dividing your email list into smaller, more targeted groups based on specific criteria. This allows you to tailor your messages to the unique preferences and behaviors of each segment, leading to higher engagement rates.

Demographic segmentation, such as age, gender, location, and job title, is a basic yet effective approach. Behavioral segmentation takes it a step further by considering factors like purchase history, website activity, and email engagement. For instance, customers who frequently open and click on your emails might be more receptive to promotional content, while those who haven't engaged recently might benefit from a re-engagement campaign.

Advanced segmentation can involve psychographic factors, such as interests, values, and lifestyle choices. This requires more in-depth data but can significantly enhance the personalization of your campaigns.

Crafting Effective Email Campaigns

Creating an effective email campaign involves more than just sending a message. It requires a strategic approach to content, design, timing, and testing.

1. Compelling Subject Lines and Preheaders

The subject line is the first thing recipients see, and it plays a critical role in whether they open your email. It should be concise, intriguing, and relevant. Personalization, such as using the recipient's name or referencing their past interactions, can increase open rates. The preheader, which is the text that appears next to or below the subject line in the inbox, should complement the subject line and provide additional incentive to open the email.

2. Engaging Content

Once the email is opened, the content must deliver on the promise of the subject line. Your emails should be valuable, relevant, and engaging. This can include a mix of informative articles, product updates, promotional offers, and personalized recommendations.

A clear and compelling call-to-action (CTA) is essential. It should guide the reader on what to do next, whether it's making a purchase, signing up for a webinar, or downloading a resource. The CTA should be prominently placed and easy to follow.

3. Visual Design and Layout

The design of your email should be visually appealing and easy to read. Use a clean, uncluttered layout with a balance of text and images. Ensure your email is mobile-friendly, as a significant portion of users will view it on their smartphones. Responsive design ensures that your email looks good on any device.

Images should be high-quality and relevant, but not so large that they slow down loading times. Use alt text for images in case they don't load, and include descriptive links and buttons to guide readers.

4. Personalization and Automation

Personalization goes beyond using the recipient's name. It involves tailoring the content based on their preferences, behaviors, and past interactions with your brand. Automated email sequences can enhance personalization by sending targeted messages at the right time. For example, welcome emails for new subscribers, birthday emails, and follow-up emails after a purchase can significantly improve engagement.

5. Timing and Frequency

The timing of your emails can greatly impact their effectiveness. Consider your audience's time zones and peak engagement times. For instance, business-related emails might perform better during weekdays, while retail promotions might see higher engagement over the weekend.

Frequency is also crucial. Sending emails too frequently can lead to unsubscribes, while infrequent emails might cause your audience to forget about you. Test different frequencies to find the optimal balance for your audience.

Measuring and Optimizing Performance

The success of your email marketing campaigns hinges on continuous measurement and optimization. This involves analyzing key metrics and making data-driven decisions to improve future campaigns.

1. Key Metrics

Open rate, click-through rate (CTR), conversion rate, and unsubscribe rate are some of the primary metrics to monitor. The open rate indicates how well your subject lines are performing, while the CTR shows the effectiveness of your content and CTA (Call to Action). The conversion rate reveals how well your emails are driving desired actions, such as sales or sign-ups. The unsubscribe rate can indicate if your frequency or content is off-putting to your audience.

2. A/B Testing

A/B testing, or split testing, involves sending two variations of an email to different segments of your audience to see which performs better. You can test various elements, such as subject lines, content, design, and CTAs. By systematically testing and analyzing results, you can make informed decisions that enhance your campaigns' effectiveness.

3. Feedback and Continuous Improvement

Soliciting feedback from your subscribers can provide valuable insights. Surveys, polls, and direct questions within your emails can help you understand their preferences and pain points. Use this feedback to continuously refine your content and strategy.

4. Compliance and Best Practices

Adhering to legal regulations and best practices is crucial for maintaining trust and avoiding penalties. Ensure that your email marketing complies with laws like GDPR and CAN-SPAM Act. This includes obtaining explicit consent from subscribers, providing clear opt-out options, and accurately representing your identity and content.

Maintaining a clean email list by regularly removing inactive subscribers and invalid email addresses is essential. Not only does this improve your deliverability rates, but it also ensures that your emails reach an engaged audience.

The Future of Email Marketing

Email marketing is continually evolving, with emerging technologies and trends shaping its future. Artificial intelligence (AI) and machine learning are becoming increasingly important in personalizing and optimizing email campaigns. Predictive analytics can help marketers anticipate customer behavior and tailor their strategies accordingly.

Interactive emails, featuring elements like carousels (rotating content displays often used on websites and apps to showcase multiple images, products, or pieces of information in a single, interactive space), quizzes, and embedded videos, are gaining popularity. These enhance engagement by allowing recipients to interact with the content directly within the email.

Integration with other digital marketing channels, such as social media and SMS, is also on the rise. A cohesive multichannel approach can enhance the overall customer experience and reinforce your messaging.

Conclusion

Email marketing remains a cornerstone of digital marketing, offering a direct, personal, and highly effective way to engage with your audience. By building and segmenting email lists, crafting compelling campaigns, and continuously measuring and optimizing performance, you can harness the full potential of this powerful tool. Adhering to best practices and staying abreast of emerging trends will ensure that your email marketing efforts remain relevant and impactful in the ever-evolving digital landscape.

Chapter 16. Influencer Marketing

Introduction

In the ever-evolving landscape of digital marketing, influencer marketing has emerged as a formidable strategy for brands seeking to expand their reach, engage with new audiences, and build credibility. By leveraging the popularity and trust that influencers have cultivated with their followers, businesses can achieve significant marketing objectives in ways that traditional advertising often cannot. This chapter explores the nuances of influencer marketing, from identifying and partnering with the right influencers to measuring the impact of these campaigns.

Identifying and Partnering with Influencers

The foundation of a successful influencer marketing campaign lies in identifying the right influencers to partner with. This process involves several critical steps to ensure that the chosen influencers align with the brand's values, target audience, and campaign goals.

1. Understanding the Audience

The first step in identifying suitable influencers is to have a deep understanding of the brand's target audience. This includes demographics such as age, gender, location, and interests. By clearly defining the audience, brands can narrow down the pool of potential influencers who have a following that matches these characteristics. For instance, a beauty brand targeting young women would benefit from partnering with beauty bloggers and makeup artists who have a significant female following in the desired age group.

2. Researching Potential Influencers

Once the target audience is defined, the next step is to research potential influencers. This can be done through various methods such as social media searches, influencer marketing platforms, and using tools like Google Alerts to monitor mentions of relevant topics. It's important to look beyond the number of followers an influencer has; engagement rates, content quality, and the influencer's relationship with their audience are equally crucial metrics. High engagement rates indicate that the influencer's followers are actively interested in their content, making them more likely to trust and act upon the influencer's recommendations.

3. Evaluating Fit and Authenticity

Authenticity is a key factor in influencer marketing. Audiences are quick to detect inauthentic partnerships, which can harm both the brand and the influencer's reputation. Therefore, it's essential to evaluate whether the influencer's content, style, and values align with the brand. This involves reviewing their past collaborations, the tone of their content, and how they interact with their followers. Authentic influencers who genuinely use and endorse the brand's products or services can create more credible and persuasive content.

4. Establishing a Relationship

Once potential influencers are identified, the next step is to reach out and establish a relationship. This involves a personalized approach, expressing genuine interest in the influencer's work and explaining why the partnership would be mutually beneficial. Clear communication about the campaign objectives, deliverables, and compensation is crucial. Building a strong relationship with influencers can lead to long-term partnerships, which are often more effective than one-off collaborations.

5. Negotiating Terms and Contracts

After an influencer expresses interest in the collaboration, the terms of the partnership need to be negotiated. This includes the type and amount of content to be created, the timeline, compensation, and any exclusivity agreements. It's important to draft a contract that outlines these details to protect both the brand and the influencer. This contract should also cover usage rights for the content, compliance with advertising regulations, and guidelines for disclosing the partnership to the audience.

Measuring the Impact of Influencer Campaigns

Measuring the effectiveness of influencer marketing campaigns is crucial to understand their impact and to refine future strategies. Unlike traditional marketing methods, influencer marketing metrics can be complex and multifaceted, requiring a comprehensive approach to evaluation.

1. Defining KPIs and Objectives

Before launching an influencer campaign, it's essential to define clear Key Performance Indicators (KPIs) and objectives. These could include brand awareness, engagement, website traffic, lead generation, or sales. Establishing specific, measurable goals provides a benchmark against which the success of the campaign can be assessed.

2. Tracking Engagement Metrics

Engagement metrics such as likes, comments, shares, and views are the most immediate indicators of how well the influencer's content is resonating with their audience. High engagement rates suggest that the audience is interested and interacting with the content, which can lead to increased brand awareness and consideration. Tools like Instagram Insights, YouTube Analytics, and third-party platforms like Hootsuite can provide detailed engagement data.

3. Analyzing Traffic and Conversion Data

To measure the direct impact of an influencer campaign on website traffic and conversions, brands can use tools like Google Analytics. By creating unique tracking links or using UTM parameters (tracking codes added to URLs), brands can track the traffic driven by influencer content. Additionally, setting up goals in Google Analytics can help measure specific actions taken by users, such as signing up for a newsletter, downloading a resource, or making a purchase. Comparing these metrics before and after the campaign provides insights into its effectiveness.

4. Assessing Return on Investment (ROI)

Calculating the ROI of an influencer marketing campaign involves comparing the revenue generated from the campaign to the costs incurred. This includes payments to influencers, production costs, and any additional expenses. ROI can be measured in terms of direct sales attributed to the campaign, as well as indirect benefits such as increased brand awareness and improved brand sentiment. Tools like affiliate marketing platforms and discount codes can help track sales and conversions directly linked to influencer efforts.

5. Monitoring Brand Sentiment

Brand sentiment analysis involves assessing the overall attitude of consumers towards the brand during and after the campaign. This can be done by monitoring social media mentions, comments, and reviews. Positive sentiment indicates that the campaign is well-received, while negative sentiment may suggest issues that need to be addressed. Sentiment analysis tools like Brandwatch and Mention can automate this process and provide valuable insights into how the campaign is impacting brand perception.

6. Evaluating Long-term Impact

Influencer marketing can have long-term benefits that extend beyond the immediate metrics. These include increased brand loyalty, a stronger online presence, and ongoing engagement with new audiences. Evaluating the long-term impact involves tracking brand performance over time and comparing it to periods before the influencer campaign. This can provide a holistic view of how influencer marketing contributes to the overall growth and success of the brand.

Best Practices and Future Trends

To maximize the effectiveness of influencer marketing, brands should adhere to best practices and stay abreast of emerging trends in the industry.

1. Building Long-term Partnerships

While one-off campaigns can be effective, building long-term partnerships with influencers can yield more substantial benefits. Long-term collaborations allow influencers to integrate the brand into their content more naturally, fostering greater trust and authenticity. This continuity can lead to deeper connections with the audience and more sustained results.

2. Diversifying Influencer Portfolios

Relying on a diverse range of influencers can help brands reach different segments of their target audience and mitigate the risks associated with over-reliance on a single influencer. This includes working with macro-influencers, micro-influencers, and even nano-influencers, each of whom can bring unique strengths to the campaign.

Macro-Influencers: Individuals with a large following (typically 100,000 to 1 million followers) on social media, known for their broad reach and strong influence across various audiences.

Micro-Influencers: Social media personalities with a moderate following (usually between 10,000 and 100,000 followers) who are considered experts within specific niches and have high engagement rates.

Nano-Influencers: Users with a small but dedicated following (often fewer than 10,000 followers), known for their close-knit and highly engaged communities, often within very specific niches or local areas.

3. Embracing Authenticity and Transparency

Authenticity and transparency are paramount in influencer marketing. Influencers should be encouraged to create content that genuinely reflects their opinions and experiences with the brand. Clear disclosure of paid partnerships is not only a legal requirement but also builds trust with the audience. Brands should collaborate with influencers to create content that feels organic and resonates with their followers.

4. Leveraging New Platforms and Technologies

As social media platforms evolve, new opportunities for influencer marketing emerge. Brands should stay informed about the latest trends and technologies, such as the rise of TikTok, live streaming, and virtual reality experiences. Experimenting with these new formats can help brands stay ahead of the curve and engage with audiences in innovative ways.

5. Focusing on Data and Analytics

Data-driven decision-making is crucial for optimizing influencer marketing strategies. Brands should leverage analytics tools to continuously monitor and analyze campaign performance. This data can inform future campaigns, helping brands refine their approach and achieve better results. Regularly reviewing metrics and gathering feedback from influencers can provide valuable insights for ongoing improvement.

Conclusion

Influencer marketing has revolutionized the way brands connect with consumers, offering a powerful alternative to traditional advertising. By carefully identifying and partnering with the right influencers, brands can amplify their message, build trust, and drive significant engagement. Measuring the impact of these campaigns through detailed analytics ensures that brands can assess their effectiveness and make informed decisions for future strategies. As the digital marketing landscape continues to evolve, embracing best practices and staying attuned to emerging trends will be essential for leveraging the full potential of influencer marketing.

Chapter 17. Affiliate Marketing

Introduction

Affiliate marketing has emerged as a powerful tool in the digital marketing arsenal, offering businesses an effective way to expand their reach and increase sales. This form of marketing leverages the influence and audience of third-party marketers, known as affiliates, who promote products or services in exchange for a commission. This symbiotic relationship benefits both the merchant and the affiliate, creating a dynamic and scalable model for growth. In this comprehensive guide, we will explore the intricacies of affiliate marketing, from building an affiliate program to managing and optimizing affiliate relationships.

Understanding Affiliate Marketing

At its core, affiliate marketing is a performance-based marketing strategy where affiliates earn a commission for driving traffic or sales to a merchant's website. This model aligns the interests of both parties: affiliates are motivated to promote products effectively, while merchants gain access to a wider audience without upfront costs. The process typically involves four key players: the merchant, the affiliate, the consumer, and the affiliate network, which acts as an intermediary to track transactions and manage payments.

Building an Affiliate Program

Creating a successful affiliate program requires careful planning and execution. The first step is to define the goals and objectives of the program. Are you looking to increase brand awareness, drive sales, or expand your customer base? Clear objectives will guide the development and management of the program.

Next, it's essential to choose the right affiliate network or software to manage the program. Popular affiliate networks like ShareASale, Commission Junction, and Rakuten provide robust platforms that facilitate tracking, reporting, and payment processes. Alternatively, businesses can opt for affiliate software solutions like Post Affiliate Pro or Tapfiliate, which offer more control and customization.

Once the platform is chosen, the next step is to design a competitive commission structure. This involves determining the percentage or amount affiliates will earn for each sale or action. The commission should be attractive enough to motivate affiliates while ensuring it remains sustainable for the business.

Recruiting affiliates is a critical phase in building your program. This can be done through various channels, including your website, email marketing, social media, and dedicated affiliate recruitment sites. Offering incentives such as higher initial commissions or performance bonuses can attract high-quality affiliates. It's also beneficial to provide affiliates with marketing materials like banners, links, and product information to help them promote effectively.

Managing and Optimizing Affiliate Relationships

Effective management of affiliate relationships is crucial for the long-term success of the program. Regular communication with affiliates helps to build trust and loyalty. This can be achieved through newsletters, webinars, and one-on-one meetings. Providing affiliates with updates on new products, promotions, and best practices keeps them engaged and informed.

Tracking and analyzing performance is vital to understand which affiliates are driving the most value. This can be done through detailed reports on traffic, sales, and commissions. Identifying top-performing affiliates allows businesses to offer additional incentives and support to maximize their efforts.

Optimization is an ongoing process in affiliate marketing. Testing different marketing strategies, commission structures, and promotional materials can help identify what works best. A/B testing, for instance, can reveal which types of creatives or landing pages convert better. Additionally, segmenting affiliates based on their performance or niche can allow for more targeted support and incentives.

Legal and Ethical Considerations

Compliance with legal and ethical standards is essential in affiliate marketing. This includes adhering to advertising regulations, such as disclosing affiliate relationships to consumers. The Federal Trade Commission (FTC) in the United States, for example, requires affiliates to disclose their financial interest in the products they promote. Ensuring transparency builds trust with consumers and protects the business from potential legal issues.

Affiliates should also be provided with clear guidelines on acceptable marketing practices. This includes prohibiting deceptive advertising, spam, and any form of fraud. Regular monitoring and enforcement of these guidelines help maintain the integrity of the program.

Case Studies and Examples

Successful affiliate marketing programs can provide valuable insights and inspiration. For instance, Amazon's affiliate program, Amazon Associates, is one of the most well-known and successful programs. It offers a wide range of products for affiliates to promote and provides detailed reports and tools to help them succeed. Amazon's approach to affiliate marketing emphasizes the importance of providing affiliates with the resources and support they need to thrive.

Another example is the Shopify Affiliate Program, which targets influencers and content creators in the e-commerce space. Shopify offers competitive commissions and extensive training resources, demonstrating the effectiveness of empowering affiliates with knowledge and support.

The Future of Affiliate Marketing

As digital marketing continues to evolve, so does affiliate marketing. Emerging technologies such as artificial intelligence (AI) and machine learning are poised to transform how affiliate programs are managed and optimized. AI can help identify high-potential affiliates, predict trends, and automate routine tasks, making the process more efficient and effective.

The rise of influencer marketing also intersects with affiliate marketing. Influencers, with their engaged audiences, can drive significant traffic and sales through affiliate links. Collaborating with influencers can enhance the reach and credibility of affiliate marketing efforts.

Moreover, the increasing importance of data privacy and security will shape the future of affiliate marketing. Businesses will need to ensure that their affiliate programs comply with data protection regulations like the General Data Protection Regulation (GDPR) in the European Union. Protecting consumer data and maintaining trust will be paramount.

Conclusion

Affiliate marketing is a versatile and powerful component of digital marketing, offering businesses a cost-effective way to expand their reach and boost sales. Building a successful affiliate program involves careful planning, effective recruitment, and ongoing management. By providing affiliates with the tools and support they need, businesses can foster strong, productive relationships.

Managing and optimizing these relationships requires continuous communication, performance analysis, and adherence to legal and ethical standards. As technology and consumer behavior continue to evolve, affiliate marketing will adapt, offering new opportunities for growth and innovation.

By understanding the fundamentals and staying abreast of emerging trends, businesses can leverage affiliate marketing to achieve their digital marketing goals. Whether you are a seasoned marketer or new to the field, the principles outlined in this article will help you navigate the dynamic landscape of affiliate marketing and harness its potential for success.

Chapter 18. Conversion Rate Optimization (CRO)

Introduction

In the rapidly evolving landscape of digital marketing, Conversion Rate Optimization (CRO) has emerged as a crucial practice for enhancing the performance and profitability of online ventures. CRO involves a systematic approach to increasing the percentage of visitors to a website who take desired actions, such as making a purchase, filling out a form, or subscribing to a newsletter. This comprehensive guide delves into the techniques for improving website conversions, the role of A/B testing, and the application of user experience (UX) principles in CRO.

Understanding Conversion Rate Optimization

Conversion Rate Optimization is the practice of improving the percentage of users who perform a desired action on a website. The desired action can vary depending on the business goals, such as completing a purchase, signing up for a service, or downloading a resource. CRO is a data-driven process that involves understanding user behavior, identifying obstacles to conversion, and implementing changes to enhance the user journey.

Effective CRO not only boosts revenue but also enhances the overall user experience, leading to higher customer satisfaction and retention. The process involves a combination of quantitative and qualitative research methods to gather insights about user interactions and preferences. By continually testing and optimizing elements of a website, businesses can achieve significant improvements in their conversion rates.

Techniques for Improving Website Conversions

Improving website conversions requires a multifaceted approach, involving various techniques and strategies. Some of the most effective methods include:

1. Enhancing Website Design and Layout

The design and layout of a website play a crucial role in guiding users towards conversion. A clean, intuitive design with a logical structure makes it easier for users to navigate and find what they are looking for. Key elements such as call-to-action (CTA) buttons, navigation menus, and content placement should be strategically designed to capture user attention and encourage action.

2. Optimizing Landing Pages

Landing pages are often the first point of contact for users, making them critical to conversion efforts. An effective landing page should be focused, relevant, and compelling. It should clearly communicate the value proposition and provide a straightforward path to conversion. Techniques such as using persuasive headlines, engaging visuals, and concise copy can significantly improve the performance of landing pages.

3. Improving Page Load Speed

Page load speed is a vital factor in user experience and conversion rates. Slow-loading pages can frustrate users and lead to higher bounce rates. Optimizing images, leveraging browser caching, and minimizing code can help improve load times. Tools like Google PageSpeed Insights can provide valuable recommendations for enhancing page speed.

4. Implementing Clear and Compelling CTAs

Call-to-action buttons are critical for guiding users towards conversion. Effective CTAs are clear, concise, and action-oriented. They should stand out visually and convey a sense of urgency or value. A/B testing different CTA designs, placements, and wording can help identify the most effective variations.

5. Leveraging Social Proof

Social proof, such as customer testimonials, reviews, and case studies, can significantly influence user decisions. Displaying social proof prominently on the website can build trust and credibility, making users more likely to convert. Including logos of reputable clients, user-generated content, and industry certifications can also enhance the perceived value of the offerings.

6. Simplifying Forms

Forms are a common element in conversion paths, whether for lead generation or checkout processes. Simplifying forms by reducing the number of fields, using clear labels, and providing real-time validation can improve form completion rates. Offering incentives, such as discounts or free resources, can also encourage users to complete forms.

A/B Testing and User Experience (UX) Principles

A/B testing and user experience (UX) principles are integral components of a successful CRO strategy. These practices allow businesses to make data-driven decisions and continually refine their websites to meet user needs and preferences.

1. A/B Testing

A/B testing, also known as split testing, involves comparing two versions of a web page or element to determine which one performs better. This method allows businesses to test different hypotheses and identify the most effective variations. Key steps in the A/B testing process include:

Hypothesis Formation: Based on user data and insights, form a hypothesis about what changes might improve conversions. For example, "Changing the CTA button color from blue to green will increase click-through rates".

Test Design: Create two versions of the web page or element - Version A (the control) and Version B (the variation). Ensure that only one element is changed to isolate its impact on performance.

Data Collection: Use tools such as Google Optimize or Optimizely to run the test and collect data on user interactions. Track metrics such as click-through rates, conversion rates, and bounce rates.

Analysis: Analyze the test results to determine whether the variation performed significantly better than the control. Use statistical significance to ensure that the results are not due to chance.

Implementation: If the variation outperforms the control, implement the changes on the live website. Continuously monitor the impact and conduct further tests as needed.

A/B testing allows for iterative optimization, enabling businesses to make incremental improvements that collectively enhance conversion rates.

2. User Experience (UX) Principles

User experience (UX) principles focus on creating a seamless and enjoyable journey for users as they interact with a website. Good UX design considers the needs, behaviors, and emotions of users, aiming to provide a positive and efficient experience. Key UX principles that impact CRO include:

Usability: A website should be easy to navigate and use. Clear menus, intuitive layouts, and consistent design elements contribute to a user-friendly experience. Conducting usability testing can identify pain points and areas for improvement.

Accessibility: Ensuring that a website is accessible to all users, including those with disabilities, is crucial for both ethical and practical reasons. Implementing features such as keyboard navigation, screen reader compatibility, and alt text for images enhances accessibility and broadens the potential user base.

Responsiveness: With the increasing use of mobile devices, responsive design is essential. A website should provide a consistent and optimized experience across different screen sizes and devices. Responsive design improves user satisfaction and can positively impact conversion rates.

Visual Hierarchy: Effective visual hierarchy guides users' attention to the most important elements on a page. Using contrasting colors, varying font sizes, and strategic placement helps prioritize content and CTAs, making it easier for users to understand and act.

Content Quality: High-quality, relevant content is a cornerstone of good UX. Content should be clear, engaging, and tailored to the target audience. Incorporating multimedia elements such as images, videos, and infographics can enhance content and keep users engaged.

Feedback and Interaction: Providing feedback to users as they interact with the website is essential for maintaining engagement. This includes visual cues for clickable elements, confirmation messages for actions, and error notifications for form inputs. Interactive elements such as sliders, hover effects, and animations can also enhance the user experience.

Conclusion

Conversion Rate Optimization (CRO) is a vital practice in the realm of digital marketing, offering a systematic approach to enhancing website performance and achieving business goals. By employing techniques such as improving website design, optimizing landing pages, enhancing page load speed, implementing clear CTAs, leveraging social proof, and simplifying forms, businesses can significantly boost their conversion rates.

A/B testing and user experience (UX) principles play pivotal roles in the CRO process. A/B testing allows for data-driven decision-making and iterative optimization, while UX principles ensure that the website provides a seamless and enjoyable experience for users. By continuously analyzing user behavior, testing hypotheses, and refining website elements, businesses can create a more effective and engaging online presence.

Ultimately, CRO is an ongoing process that requires a commitment to understanding and meeting the needs of users. By integrating CRO practices into their digital marketing strategies, businesses can not only improve conversions but also build lasting relationships with their customers, driving long-term success and growth.

Chapter 19. E-commerce Strategies

Introduction

In the digital age, e-commerce has emerged as a pivotal component of the business landscape, revolutionizing the way goods and services are bought and sold. The rise of online retail has been driven by the convenience, accessibility, and efficiency it offers both businesses and consumers. However, succeeding in the e-commerce space requires more than just setting up an online store. It demands strategic planning, a deep understanding of the market, and the ability to leverage technology effectively. This chapter explores the key e-commerce strategies essential for building a thriving online retail business, focusing on best practices and the utilization of platforms like Shopify and WooCommerce.

Understanding the E-commerce Ecosystem

The e-commerce ecosystem encompasses a wide range of activities and processes, from the initial creation of an online store to the management of logistics and customer service. To navigate this complex environment, businesses must adopt a holistic approach that integrates various aspects of digital marketing, technology, and consumer behavior. A successful e-commerce strategy begins with a clear understanding of the target market and the competitive landscape. This involves researching consumer preferences, identifying market trends, and analyzing the strengths and weaknesses of competitors.

Best Practices for Online Retail

One of the fundamental best practices for online retail is ensuring a seamless and intuitive user experience. The design and functionality of an e-commerce website play a crucial role in attracting and retaining customers. A well-designed website should be visually appealing, easy to navigate, and optimized for mobile devices. Given the increasing use of smartphones for online shopping, mobile optimization is no longer optional but a necessity. Websites that load quickly and offer a smooth browsing experience on mobile devices are more likely to convert visitors into customers.

Another critical aspect of online retail is product presentation. High-quality images, detailed descriptions, and customer reviews can significantly influence purchasing decisions. Investing in professional photography and providing comprehensive information about products can help build trust and credibility with potential buyers. Additionally, incorporating user-generated content, such as reviews and testimonials, can enhance the authenticity of the brand and foster a sense of community among customers.

Pricing strategy is another key element that can make or break an e-commerce business. Competitive pricing, along with attractive offers and discounts, can drive sales and encourage repeat purchases. However, it's important to balance affordability with profitability. Dynamic pricing, which adjusts prices based on demand and competition, can be an effective way to maximize revenue.

Customer service is a cornerstone of e-commerce success. Providing excellent customer support through various channels, such as live chat, email, and social media, can improve customer satisfaction and loyalty. Implementing a robust return and refund policy is also essential to build trust and mitigate the risk of abandoned purchases.

Leveraging Technology Platforms

Technology platforms like Shopify and WooCommerce have democratized e-commerce by making it accessible to businesses of all sizes. These platforms offer a range of features and tools that simplify the process of setting up and managing an online store.

Shopify is a hosted e-commerce platform that provides an all-in-one solution for online retail. It offers a user-friendly interface, customizable templates, and a range of integrated features such as payment processing, inventory management, and marketing tools. One of the key advantages of Shopify is its scalability, which allows businesses to grow without worrying about technical complexities. Shopify also supports a wide range of third-party apps and integrations, enabling businesses to enhance their store's functionality and streamline operations.

To maximize the benefits of Shopify, businesses should take advantage of its SEO features to improve their search engine rankings. This includes optimizing product titles, descriptions, and meta tags, as well as using analytics tools to track and analyze website traffic. Additionally, Shopify's abandoned cart recovery feature can help recover lost sales by sending automated emails to customers who leave items in their cart without completing the purchase.

WooCommerce, on the other hand, is an open-source e-commerce plugin for WordPress. It offers a high level of customization and flexibility, making it an ideal choice for businesses with specific requirements or those looking to create a unique online store. WooCommerce is free to use, but businesses may need to invest in additional plugins and themes to unlock its full potential.

One of the strengths of WooCommerce is its integration with WordPress, which allows businesses to leverage the powerful content management capabilities of the platform. By creating valuable content, such as blog posts and articles, businesses can drive organic traffic to their store and improve their SEO performance. WooCommerce also offers a range of extensions for payment gateways, shipping methods, and marketing tools, enabling businesses to tailor their store to their specific needs.

Marketing and Promotion Strategies

Effective marketing and promotion are critical to driving traffic and sales in the e-commerce space. A multi-channel approach that combines various digital marketing tactics can help businesses reach a wider audience and achieve their sales goals.

Search Engine Optimization (SEO) is one of the most important strategies for increasing organic traffic to an e-commerce site. By optimizing product pages and content for relevant keywords, businesses can improve their visibility on search engines and attract potential customers. SEO efforts should be complemented by content marketing, which involves creating valuable and engaging content that resonates with the target audience.

Social media marketing is another powerful tool for promoting an e-commerce business. Platforms like Facebook, Instagram, and Pinterest offer a range of advertising options and features that can help businesses reach their target audience. Engaging with customers on social media, sharing user-generated content, and running targeted ad campaigns can drive traffic and increase brand awareness.

Email marketing remains one of the most effective ways to nurture customer relationships and drive repeat sales. By building a mailing list and sending personalized and relevant emails, businesses can keep customers informed about new products, promotions, and other updates. Segmenting the email list based on customer behavior and preferences can further enhance the effectiveness of email campaigns.

Paid advertising, such as Google Ads and social media ads, can provide an immediate boost to traffic and sales. By targeting specific keywords and demographics, businesses can reach potential customers who are actively searching for their products. Retargeting ads, which target users who have previously visited the website, can also help recover lost sales and increase conversion rates.

Analytics and Performance Monitoring

To ensure the success of an e-commerce strategy, businesses must continuously monitor and analyze their performance. This involves tracking key metrics such as traffic, conversion rates, average order value, and customer lifetime value. *Average order value* is the average amount of money spent each time a customer places an order on a website or in-store. *Customer lifetime value* is the total revenue a business can expect from a single customer over the course of their entire relationship.

Tools like Google Analytics and the analytics features offered by e-commerce platforms can provide valuable insights into customer behavior and the effectiveness of marketing efforts.

By analyzing this data, businesses can identify areas for improvement and make informed decisions to optimize their strategy. For example, if the data shows a high cart abandonment rate, businesses can investigate potential issues with the checkout process and implement solutions to reduce friction. Similarly, analyzing the performance of marketing campaigns can help businesses allocate their budget more effectively and focus on the channels that deliver the best results.

Conclusion

E-commerce is a dynamic and rapidly evolving field that offers tremendous opportunities for businesses willing to embrace digital transformation. By adopting best practices for online retail, leveraging technology platforms like Shopify and WooCommerce, and implementing effective marketing and promotion strategies, businesses can build a successful online store that meets the needs of today's consumers. Continuous monitoring and analysis of performance metrics are essential to staying competitive and achieving long-term success in the e-commerce space. As the digital landscape continues to evolve, businesses must remain agile and adaptable, always ready to explore new strategies and technologies to stay ahead of the curve.

Chapter 20. Mobile Marketing

Introduction

Mobile marketing is a critical component of digital marketing, reflecting the widespread adoption and use of smartphones and tablets in everyday life. This chapter will explore the intricacies of mobile marketing, providing an understanding of how to optimize for mobile devices, and delving into effective mobile app marketing strategies. Mobile marketing is not just an option; it is an essential aspect of any comprehensive digital marketing strategy.

The Rise of Mobile Marketing

The exponential growth of mobile device usage has fundamentally transformed how businesses reach and engage with their audiences. As of 2024, over 7.2 billion people use smartphones worldwide, making mobile devices the primary means of accessing the internet for many users. This shift has necessitated a paradigm change in marketing strategies, pushing businesses to prioritize mobile-friendly content and experiences. Mobile marketing encompasses a range of practices, from optimizing websites for mobile viewing to developing and promoting mobile applications.

Optimizing for Mobile Devices

Optimizing for mobile devices is crucial for ensuring that your content is accessible and engaging for users on smartphones and tablets. This optimization involves several key practices.

1. Mobile-Friendly Websites

Creating a mobile-friendly website is the first step in optimizing for mobile devices. A mobile-friendly website is designed to work well on smaller screens, providing a seamless user experience. This involves responsive design, which ensures that the website adjusts its layout and content based on the screen size of the device. Responsive design eliminates the need for separate mobile and desktop versions of a website, streamlining the management process and ensuring consistency across devices.

2. Speed and Performance

Mobile users expect fast-loading websites. Slow loading times can lead to high bounce rates, where users leave the site before it fully loads. To enhance speed and performance, it is essential to minimize the use of heavy graphics and multimedia, leverage browser caching, and optimize images and videos. Using Accelerated Mobile Pages (AMP) can also significantly improve loading times, providing a smoother experience for users. AMP is an open-source initiative by Google to optimize web pages for fast loading on mobile devices.

3. Simplified Navigation

Simplified navigation is another critical aspect of mobile optimization. Mobile users benefit from intuitive and straightforward navigation structures, as complex menus and numerous links can be cumbersome on small screens. Implementing easy-to-use navigation bars, clear call-to-action buttons, and concise menus helps users find what they need quickly and efficiently.

4. Mobile SEO

Mobile Search Engine Optimization (SEO) is vital for ensuring that your website ranks well in mobile search results. Mobile SEO involves optimizing content for local searches, as many mobile users search for services and products in their vicinity. Utilizing local keywords, creating location-specific content, and claiming and optimizing Google My Business listings are effective strategies for improving mobile SEO. Additionally, ensuring that your website is mobile-friendly is a key ranking factor in Google's mobile-first indexing approach.

Mobile App Marketing Strategies

In addition to optimizing websites for mobile devices, developing and marketing mobile applications can offer unique opportunities for engaging with your audience. Mobile apps provide a direct channel to users, enabling personalized interactions and fostering brand loyalty. Effective mobile app marketing involves several strategic approaches.

1. App Store Optimization (ASO)

App Store Optimization (ASO) is the process of optimizing mobile apps to rank higher in app store search results. ASO is akin to SEO for websites but is specific to app stores like Apple's App Store and Google Play. Key elements of ASO include choosing the right keywords, optimizing the app title and description, and using compelling visuals such as app icons and screenshots. Positive user reviews and high ratings also play a significant role in ASO, as they influence both visibility and user trust.

2. User Acquisition Strategies

Acquiring users is a primary goal of mobile app marketing. Effective user acquisition strategies include paid advertising, social media marketing, and influencer partnerships. Paid advertising on platforms like Facebook, Instagram, and Google Ads can target specific demographics and interests, driving app downloads. Social media marketing leverages the power of social networks to create buzz and attract users. Collaborating with influencers who have a substantial following can also be a powerful way to promote an app, as recommendations from trusted figures can significantly impact user decisions.

3. In-App Engagement and Retention

Once users have downloaded an app, keeping them engaged is crucial for long-term success. In-app engagement strategies involve creating a compelling user experience that encourages regular use. This can be achieved through personalized content, push notifications, and gamification (the application of game-design elements and principles in non-game contexts to enhance user engagement and motivation). Push notifications, when used judiciously, can remind users of important updates or encourage them to return to the app. Gamification elements, such as rewards, challenges, and leaderboards, can make the app more interactive and enjoyable.

4. Analyzing User Behavior

Understanding how users interact with an app is essential for optimizing the user experience and improving retention rates. Mobile analytics tools can track user behavior, providing insights into how users navigate the app, which features they use most, and where they drop off. Analyzing this data helps identify areas for improvement and informs decisions on updates and new features. By continuously refining the app based on user feedback and behavior, businesses can enhance user satisfaction and loyalty.

5. Monetization Strategies

Monetizing a mobile app is a critical aspect of mobile app marketing. There are several monetization strategies, including in-app purchases, subscription models, advertising, and freemium models. In-app purchases allow users to buy virtual goods or additional features within the app. Subscription models provide ongoing revenue through regular payments for premium content or services. Advertising can be integrated into the app, generating revenue from third-party ads. Freemium models offer a basic version of the app for free, with additional features available for purchase. Choosing the right monetization strategy depends on the app's purpose and target audience.

6. Cross-Promotion and Partnerships

Cross-promotion and partnerships can extend the reach of a mobile app and attract new users. Cross-promotion involves promoting the app across different platforms, such as social media, email newsletters, and other apps. Partnerships with complementary businesses or influencers can introduce the app to new audiences and create mutually beneficial relationships. For instance, a fitness app could partner with a health and wellness brand to offer exclusive discounts or content, attracting users from both audiences.

The Future of Mobile Marketing

The landscape of mobile marketing is continually evolving, driven by technological advancements and changing user behaviors. Emerging technologies such as augmented reality (AR), virtual reality (VR), and artificial intelligence (AI) are shaping the future of mobile marketing, offering new ways to engage with users and create immersive experiences.

1. Augmented Reality (AR) and Virtual Reality (VR)

AR and VR technologies are transforming how users interact with mobile content. AR overlays digital information onto the real world, enhancing the user's environment. This can be used in marketing to create interactive and engaging experiences, such as virtual try-ons for fashion brands or interactive product demonstrations. VR provides fully immersive experiences, transporting users to virtual environments. While VR requires specialized equipment, mobile VR solutions are becoming more accessible, allowing users to explore virtual spaces using their smartphones.

2. Artificial Intelligence (AI) and Machine Learning (ML)

AI and ML are revolutionizing mobile marketing by enabling more personalized and efficient interactions. AI-powered chatbots can provide instant customer support, answering queries and guiding users through the app. ML algorithms can analyze user data to deliver personalized content and recommendations, enhancing the user experience. Predictive analytics can anticipate user needs and behaviors, allowing businesses to tailor their marketing strategies accordingly.

3. 5G Technology

The rollout of 5G technology is set to revolutionize mobile marketing by offering faster speeds, lower latency (the delay between a user's action and the response from a system or server), and increased connectivity. 5G will enhance the capabilities of mobile devices, enabling more sophisticated applications and real-time interactions. For marketers, 5G opens up new possibilities for delivering high-quality, data-intensive content, such as live streaming, interactive ads, and immersive AR/VR experiences.

4. Privacy and Data Security

As mobile marketing evolves, concerns around privacy and data security continue to grow. Users are increasingly aware of how their data is being used and are demanding greater transparency and control. Compliance with data protection regulations, such as the General Data Protection Regulation (GDPR) and the California Consumer Privacy Act (CCPA), is essential for maintaining user trust. Businesses must prioritize data security, implement robust privacy policies, and provide clear communication about data collection and usage practices.

Conclusion

Mobile marketing is an indispensable element of a comprehensive digital marketing strategy. The widespread use of mobile devices has transformed how businesses connect with their audiences, necessitating a focus on mobile-friendly websites and effective mobile app marketing strategies. By optimizing for mobile devices, leveraging app store optimization, and employing user acquisition and engagement tactics, businesses can enhance their mobile presence and drive success. As technology continues to evolve, staying abreast of emerging trends and prioritizing privacy and data security will be crucial for navigating the future of mobile marketing.

Chapter 21. Video Marketing

Introduction

In the sprawling landscape of digital marketing, video marketing has emerged as a powerful and indispensable tool. With the rise of high-speed internet and the ubiquity of mobile devices, video content has become more accessible and more engaging than ever before. This chapter delves into the intricacies of video marketing, exploring the creation of engaging content and the strategies for effective distribution across various platforms.

The Power of Video Marketing

Video marketing leverages the compelling nature of video to capture attention, convey messages, and drive engagement. Videos combine visual and auditory elements to create a dynamic storytelling medium that can evoke emotions and build connections with audiences more effectively than text or static images. Whether it's a short, catchy advertisement, an in-depth tutorial, or a live stream, videos can deliver complex information in an easily digestible and entertaining format.

Creating Engaging Video Content

Creating engaging video content is an art and a science. It requires a deep understanding of your audience, a clear message, and a creative approach to storytelling.

1. Know Your Audience

Understanding your audience is the first step in creating engaging video content. Conduct thorough research to identify the demographics, preferences, and behaviors of your target audience. What are their pain points? What kind of content do they consume and share? By answering these questions, you can tailor your videos to resonate with your audience's interests and needs.

2. Crafting the Message

A clear and compelling message is at the heart of every successful video. Whether you're promoting a product, educating your audience, or simply entertaining them, your message should be concise and impactful. Start with a strong hook to grab attention in the first few seconds. Use storytelling techniques to build a narrative that keeps viewers engaged until the end. Remember, the goal is not just to inform but also to inspire and motivate action.

3. Visual and Auditory Elements

The visual and auditory elements of a video are critical in creating an engaging experience. High-quality visuals, including sharp images, vibrant colors, and smooth transitions, can captivate viewers. Similarly, clear and crisp audio, complemented by appropriate background music and sound effects, enhances the overall viewing experience. Invest in good equipment and post-production software to ensure your videos look and sound professional.

4. Length and Format

The length and format of your video should align with the platform and the viewing habits of your audience. Shorter videos (30 seconds to 2 minutes) are ideal for social media platforms where attention spans are shorter. For educational content or tutorials, longer formats (5 to 20 minutes) might be more appropriate. Consider experimenting with different formats such as live videos, animations, and interactive videos to keep your content fresh and engaging.

Platforms and Distribution Strategies

Creating great video content is only half the battle. The other half is getting your videos in front of the right audience. Effective distribution strategies involve choosing the right platforms and optimizing your videos for maximum reach and engagement.

1. YouTube: The Behemoth of Video Platforms

YouTube is the second largest search engine in the world, making it an essential platform for video marketing. To succeed on YouTube, focus on creating high-quality content that provides value to your audience. Optimize your videos with relevant keywords, compelling titles, and detailed descriptions. Thumbnails are also crucial as they act as the visual trigger for clicks; make sure they are attractive and representative of your content. Additionally, engage with your audience through comments and community posts to build a loyal following.

2. Social Media: The Viral Potential

Social media platforms like Facebook, Instagram, and TikTok offer immense potential for viral video marketing. Each platform has its unique features and audience preferences. On Facebook, longer videos tend to perform well, especially if they tell a compelling story or provide in-depth information. Instagram is ideal for short, visually striking videos, and its Stories and Reels features offer opportunities for creative and spontaneous content. TikTok, with its short-form video format, is perfect for quick, engaging content that can easily go viral. Leverage each platform's strengths and tailor your content accordingly.

3. LinkedIn: Professional and Educational Content

LinkedIn is the go-to platform for B2B marketing (the process of promoting products or services to other businesses rather than to individual consumers) and professional content. Videos that perform well on LinkedIn are often educational, industry-specific, and thought-provoking. Webinars, expert interviews, and case studies are excellent formats for this platform. Ensure your videos are professional in appearance and tone, as LinkedIn's audience is typically more discerning and focused on professional growth.

4. Website and Email Integration

Integrating videos into your website and email campaigns can significantly enhance user engagement and conversion rates. On your website, use videos to explain products, showcase testimonials, or provide tutorials. This not only keeps visitors on your site longer but also helps in building trust and credibility. In email marketing, including videos in your campaigns can increase open rates and click-through rates. Use videos to deliver personalized messages, announce new products, or offer exclusive content.

5. SEO and Video

Optimizing your videos for search engines (SEO) can significantly boost their visibility. Use relevant keywords in your video titles, descriptions, and tags. Transcribe your videos (convert spoken words and audio content from videos into written text) and include the text on your webpage to enhance searchability. Create compelling thumbnails and include closed captions to make your videos more accessible. Additionally, embedding videos on your website can improve your site's SEO by increasing the time visitors spend on your page. *Embedding videos* is the process of integrating video content into a web page so that it can be viewed directly on the site without redirecting to another platform.

Measuring Success and Iteration

To ensure your video marketing efforts are effective, it's crucial to measure performance and iterate based on the data. Key metrics to track include views, engagement (likes, comments, shares), click-through rates, and conversion rates. Use analytics tools provided by platforms like YouTube and Facebook to gain insights into how your videos are performing.

1. Analyzing Performance

Regularly analyze the performance of your videos to understand what works and what doesn't. Look for patterns in the data: which videos have the highest engagement? What types of content lead to the most conversions? Use this information to refine your content strategy and create videos that better meet the needs and preferences of your audience.

2. A/B Testing

A/B testing involves creating two versions of a video with slight variations to see which performs better. This could involve testing different thumbnails, titles, or even video lengths. By systematically testing and comparing different elements, you can optimize your videos for better performance.

3. Feedback and Adaptation

Finally, don't underestimate the value of feedback from your audience. Pay attention to comments, messages, and reviews. Engage with your viewers and ask for their opinions on what they liked or didn't like about your videos. Use this feedback to continuously improve and adapt your content strategy.

The Future of Video Marketing

The future of video marketing is poised for exciting advancements. With the rise of technologies such as virtual reality (VR), augmented reality (AR), and interactive videos, the possibilities for creating immersive and engaging content are expanding. VR and AR can offer unique, interactive experiences that were previously unimaginable. Interactive videos, where viewers can choose different paths or outcomes, can enhance engagement and provide a personalized viewing experience.

Additionally, the integration of artificial intelligence (AI) in video marketing is set to revolutionize the industry. AI can be used to analyze viewer data and preferences, enabling marketers to create highly targeted and personalized video content. AI-powered tools can also automate video editing, making the production process more efficient.

Conclusion

Video marketing is a dynamic and powerful tool in the digital marketing arsenal. By creating engaging content, leveraging the right platforms, and continually measuring and refining your strategies, you can harness the full potential of video to connect with your audience, drive engagement, and achieve your marketing goals. As technology continues to evolve, staying ahead of trends and embracing new innovations will be key to maintaining a competitive edge in the ever-changing landscape of video marketing.

Chapter 22. Local SEO

Introduction

In the rapidly evolving digital landscape, businesses must adopt dynamic strategies to remain competitive. One such essential strategy is Local Search Engine Optimization (Local SEO). Local SEO is the practice of optimizing a business's online presence to attract more business from relevant local searches. This involves various tactics and techniques that help improve a business's visibility on search engines when potential customers in the vicinity search for products or services it offers.

Understanding Local SEO

Local SEO focuses on improving search engine visibility for businesses that serve customers face-to-face in specific geographic areas. This includes brick-and-mortar businesses like restaurants, retail stores, and service-based businesses like plumbers and electricians. The goal is to make it easy for potential customers to find your business when they search online, thereby increasing foot traffic and sales. *Foot traffic* refers to the number of people walking into a specific location or area, often used to measure the popularity or potential sales of a business.

Search engines like Google use various factors to determine local search rankings. These factors include the proximity of the business to the searcher, the relevance of the business to the search query, and the prominence of the business in its local area. By optimizing these factors, businesses can improve their chances of appearing in local search results.

Strategies for Improving Local Search Visibility

Improving local search visibility involves a multifaceted approach. Here are some key strategies.

1. Optimize Your Website for Local Searches: This involves including local keywords in your website content, meta descriptions, and titles. For example, if you run a bakery in New York, use phrases like "New York bakery" or "best bakery in New York" throughout your website. Ensure your website has a clear and accurate address and contact information, ideally in a consistent format across all web pages.

2. Create Local Content: Engaging, locally-focused content can significantly boost your local SEO. Write blog posts about local events, news, or activities relevant to your business. This not only helps in attracting local readers but also signals to search engines that your business is an active part of the local community.

3. Mobile Optimization: With the increasing use of smartphones, it's crucial to ensure your website is mobile-friendly. Google's mobile-first indexing means that the mobile version of your website is considered the primary version. A responsive design and fast loading times are critical for maintaining good mobile performance and improving local search rankings.

4. Local Link Building: Building backlinks from other reputable local businesses or community websites can enhance your website's authority. Participate in local sponsorships, partnerships, or community events to earn these links. Additionally, engaging in local forums and online groups can help establish your business within the local digital community.

5. Customer Reviews and Ratings: Positive reviews and ratings play a significant role in local SEO. Encourage satisfied customers to leave reviews on your Google My Business (GMB) profile, Yelp, and other review platforms. Responding to reviews, whether positive or negative, shows that you value customer feedback and are committed to improving your services.

Leveraging Google My Business

Google My Business (GMB) is a free tool that allows businesses to manage their online presence across Google, including Search and Maps. An optimized GMB profile can significantly enhance local SEO efforts. Here's how to leverage GMB effectively.

1. Complete Your Profile: Ensure that your GMB profile is fully completed with accurate and up-to-date information. This includes your business name, address, phone number, website, and business hours. The more detailed your profile, the better it is for your local search ranking.

2. Choose the Right Categories: Selecting the appropriate categories for your business helps Google understand what your business offers and match it with relevant searches. Be as specific as possible; instead of just "restaurant", you might choose "Italian restaurant" if that's your specialty.

3. Add High-Quality Photos: Photos can make your GMB listing more appealing and informative. Add high-quality images of your business's interior, exterior, products, and services. This not only enhances your profile but also helps potential customers get a better sense of what to expect.

4. Regular Posts and Updates: Use the GMB posts feature to share updates, offers, events, and news about your business. Regularly posting on GMB can increase your visibility and keep your audience engaged.

5. Encourage and Respond to Reviews: As mentioned earlier, reviews are crucial for local SEO. Promptly respond to reviews to show customers that you value their feedback. Positive interactions can enhance your business's reputation and encourage more customers to leave reviews.

Local Citations

Local citations are online mentions of your business name, address, and phone number (NAP) on websites, directories, and social media platforms. They play a vital role in local SEO by helping search engines verify the legitimacy and accuracy of your business information. Here's how to manage local citations effectively.

1. Consistent NAP Information: Ensure that your business's NAP information is consistent across all online platforms. Inconsistencies can confuse search engines and negatively impact your local search rankings. Use the same format for your address, and regularly check and update your listings.

2. Claim and Optimize Local Listings: Claim your business listings on major local directories like Yelp, Bing Places, and industry-specific directories. Complete these profiles with as much detail as possible and include high-quality images and descriptions.

3. Use Structured Data Markup: Structured Data Markup is a standardized format for providing information about a page and classifying the page content, often used to enhance search engine understanding and display of the page in search results. Implement structured data markup (Schema.org) on your website to help search engines understand your business information better. This can improve the way your business is displayed in search results and enhance your local SEO efforts.

4. Monitor and Manage Citations: **Regularly monitor your citations to ensure they remain accurate and up-to-date. Tools like Moz Local, BrightLocal, and Whitespark can help track and manage your citations efficiently.**

Engaging with the Local Community

Building strong relationships within your local community can also boost your local SEO efforts. Participating in local events, sponsoring community activities, and collaborating with other local businesses can increase your visibility and generate local backlinks. Additionally, engaging on local social media groups and forums can help establish your presence in the local digital community.

The Importance of Analytics and Monitoring

Tracking and analyzing your local SEO efforts is crucial for continuous improvement. Use tools like Google Analytics, Google Search Console, and local SEO-specific tools to monitor your performance. Key metrics to track include website traffic, search rankings, click-through rates, and conversions from local searches. Regular analysis can help you identify areas for improvement and adjust your strategies accordingly.

Future Trends in Local SEO

Local SEO is constantly evolving, and staying updated with the latest trends is essential for maintaining a competitive edge. Some emerging trends to watch include the increasing importance of voice search, the growing use of artificial intelligence in search algorithms, and the integration of augmented reality in local search experiences. Adapting to these trends and incorporating them into your local SEO strategy can help you stay ahead of the competition.

Conclusion

Local SEO is a critical component of a comprehensive digital marketing strategy. By optimizing your website, leveraging Google My Business, managing local citations, and engaging with the local community, you can significantly improve your local search visibility. Staying informed about the latest trends and continuously monitoring your performance will ensure your local SEO efforts remain effective. As the digital landscape continues to evolve, businesses that prioritize local SEO will be better positioned to attract local customers and achieve long-term success.

Chapter 23. PHP Programming for Digital Marketers

Introduction

In the ever-evolving world of digital marketing, staying ahead of the curve often means leveraging the right tools and technologies. One such powerful tool is PHP, a server-side scripting language that has been instrumental in shaping the internet as we know it. While PHP is predominantly seen as a developer's domain, digital marketers can also harness its capabilities to enhance their strategies, streamline processes, and ultimately, drive better results.

Basics of PHP Programming

PHP, which stands for Hypertext Preprocessor, is a widely-used open-source scripting language that is particularly suited for web development and can be embedded into HTML. PHP scripts are executed on the server, and the result is returned to the browser as plain HTML. This capability allows PHP to generate dynamic page content, manage databases, handle form data, and even track user sessions.

To understand PHP basics, let's consider a simple PHP script:

```
<?php
echo "Hello, World!";
?>
```

In this script, <?php and ?> are PHP tags that indicate the start and end of a PHP code block. The echo statement outputs the string "Hello, World!" to the browser. This simplicity is one of the reasons PHP is favored by beginners and experts alike.

PHP also supports complex operations like loops, conditionals, and functions, allowing for the creation of intricate and responsive web applications. For instance, a PHP script can fetch data from a database, process it, and display it in a user-friendly format, making it a crucial tool for dynamic website development.

Enhancing Digital Marketing Efforts with PHP

For digital marketers, PHP can offer several advantages that help in crafting more effective campaigns and improving operational efficiency. Here are some ways PHP can be utilized to enhance digital marketing efforts.

1. Dynamic Content Generation

One of the most powerful features of PHP is its ability to create dynamic content. Unlike static content that remains the same for all users, dynamic content changes based on user interactions or other factors. For digital marketers, this means being able to deliver personalized experiences to users, which can significantly increase engagement and conversion rates.

For example, an e-commerce site can use PHP to display personalized product recommendations based on a user's browsing history. By leveraging PHP to pull data from the user's past interactions, marketers can tailor the content to meet individual preferences, thereby enhancing the user experience and boosting sales.

2. Efficient Data Management

Data is the backbone of digital marketing. Managing this data efficiently can be a game-changer. PHP, with its robust database connectivity, allows marketers to collect, store, and analyze vast amounts of data seamlessly. Whether it's customer information, sales data, or user interactions, PHP can interact with databases like MySQL to manage this data effectively.

Using PHP, marketers can create custom dashboards to track campaign performance in real-time. For instance, a PHP-based script can fetch and display key performance indicators (KPIs) such as website traffic, conversion rates, and user engagement metrics. This real-time data visibility enables marketers to make informed decisions quickly and adapt their strategies as needed.

3. Automated Marketing Processes

Automation is a key aspect of modern digital marketing. PHP can be used to automate repetitive tasks, saving time and reducing errors. For instance, PHP scripts can automate email marketing campaigns, schedule social media posts, or even handle lead generation and follow-up processes.

A common application of PHP in email marketing is creating personalized email campaigns. PHP can pull data from a database to customize each email with the recipient's name, purchase history, or preferences, making the communication more relevant and effective. Additionally, PHP can schedule these emails to be sent at optimal times, ensuring maximum reach and engagement.

4. Integration with Other Tools

PHP's flexibility allows it to integrate seamlessly with other marketing tools and platforms. Whether it's connecting with CRM (Customer Relationship Management) systems, analytics tools, or social media platforms, PHP can act as a bridge, facilitating smooth data flow and enhancing overall marketing efficiency.

For example, PHP can be used to integrate a website with Google Analytics. By embedding PHP scripts into web pages, marketers can track user behavior, gather insights, and analyze the effectiveness of different marketing strategies. This integration helps in creating data-driven campaigns that are more likely to succeed.

5. Enhancing User Experience

User experience (UX) is crucial for digital marketing success. A website that is slow, difficult to navigate, or unresponsive can drive potential customers away. PHP can be used to enhance the UX by ensuring websites are fast, responsive, and easy to navigate.

PHP's ability to manage sessions and cookies allows for the creation of a more personalized and seamless user experience. For instance, PHP can remember user preferences and settings, making subsequent visits more enjoyable and convenient. Additionally, PHP can be used to develop interactive features such as forms, surveys, and quizzes that engage users and encourage them to spend more time on the site.

6. SEO Optimization

Search engine optimization (SEO) is a critical component of digital marketing. PHP can play a significant role in enhancing a website's SEO performance. By generating clean and readable URLs, optimizing page load times, and creating dynamic meta tags, PHP can help improve a site's search engine ranking.

For instance, PHP can be used to create SEO-friendly URLs by rewriting dynamic URLs into more descriptive and keyword-rich ones. This not only makes the URLs more user-friendly but also helps search engines understand the content of the pages better. Moreover, PHP scripts can automatically generate meta tags based on page content, ensuring that each page is optimized for relevant keywords.

Practical Applications for Digital Marketers

To illustrate the practical applications of PHP in digital marketing, let's consider a few scenarios.

Scenario 1: Personalized Landing Pages

A digital marketer wants to create personalized landing pages for a campaign targeting different customer segments. Using PHP, they can dynamically generate landing pages that cater to specific demographics, interests, or behaviors. For example, a landing page for returning customers might display special offers based on their previous purchases, while a page for new visitors might highlight the company's unique selling points.

Scenario 2: Real-Time Analytics Dashboard

A marketing team needs to monitor the performance of their campaigns in real-time. By leveraging PHP, they can build a custom analytics dashboard that pulls data from various sources, such as Google Analytics, social media platforms, and CRM systems. This dashboard provides a comprehensive view of all key metrics, enabling the team to make data-driven decisions and adjust their strategies on the fly.

Scenario 3: Automated Lead Nurturing

A company wants to nurture leads through personalized email campaigns. PHP can be used to automate this process by sending targeted emails based on user behavior. For instance, if a user abandons their shopping cart, a PHP script can trigger an email reminder with a discount offer. This automation ensures timely and relevant communication, increasing the chances of converting leads into customers.

Scenario 4: Social Media Integration

A digital marketer wants to integrate social media feeds into their website to boost engagement. Using PHP, they can fetch and display the latest posts from platforms like X (Twitter), Facebook, and Instagram. This integration not only keeps the website content fresh and engaging but also encourages visitors to follow and interact with the brand on social media.

Conclusion

PHP programming offers a wealth of opportunities for digital marketers looking to enhance their strategies and achieve better results. From creating dynamic content and automating processes to integrating with other tools and improving SEO, PHP can significantly boost a marketer's capabilities. By understanding the basics of PHP and exploring its practical applications, digital marketers can unlock new potential in their campaigns and stay ahead in the competitive landscape of digital marketing. As technology continues to evolve, mastering tools like PHP will be essential for marketers aiming to deliver personalized, efficient, and impactful experiences to their audience.

Chapter 24. Fundamentals of Management Consulting in the Digital Age

Introduction

In an era where digital transformation is revolutionizing industries, management consulting has evolved to meet the demands of a rapidly changing business landscape. The digital age has brought about significant shifts in how companies operate, compete, and grow. As a result, management consulting has had to adapt its principles, practices, and methodologies to guide organizations through the complexities of digital transformation. This chapter explores the fundamentals of management consulting in the digital age, focusing on key principles, practices, and the impact of digital transformation.

Key Principles and Practices

1. Understanding Client Needs and Context

One of the core principles of management consulting is a deep understanding of client needs and the specific context in which they operate. This principle has become even more critical in the digital age, where industries are undergoing rapid and unpredictable changes. Consultants must immerse themselves in the client's industry, comprehend their unique challenges, and identify opportunities for digital innovation. This involves extensive research, stakeholder interviews, and market analysis to provide tailored solutions that align with the client's strategic goals.

2. Data-Driven Decision Making

In the digital era, data is a powerful asset that drives decision-making. Management consultants must leverage data analytics to provide actionable insights and recommendations. This involves collecting and analyzing large volumes of data from various sources, including customer interactions, market trends, and operational processes. By employing advanced analytics tools and techniques, consultants can uncover patterns, predict future trends, and support clients in making informed decisions that enhance efficiency, profitability, and competitiveness.

3. Agility and Adaptability

The pace of change in the digital age necessitates a high degree of agility and adaptability in management consulting. Traditional consulting methodologies often follow a linear and structured approach, which may not be suitable for the dynamic nature of digital transformation. Modern consultants must embrace agile methodologies, such as Scrum and Lean, which promote iterative development, continuous feedback, and rapid prototyping. This approach allows consultants to respond quickly to emerging challenges and opportunities, ensuring that their strategies remain relevant and effective.

4. Collaborative Approach

Collaboration is a cornerstone of effective management consulting in the digital age. Consultants must work closely with clients, fostering a partnership based on trust and mutual respect. This collaborative approach involves engaging with stakeholders at all levels of the organization, from executives to frontline employees, to gain diverse perspectives and insights. By involving clients in the consulting process, consultants can co-create solutions that are more likely to be accepted and successfully implemented.

5. Innovation and Creativity

Digital transformation requires innovative and creative thinking to identify new business models, products, and services. Management consultants must inspire and facilitate innovation within client organizations. This can involve conducting innovation workshops, ideation sessions, and design thinking exercises to generate novel ideas and solutions. Consultants should also stay abreast of emerging technologies and industry trends to provide clients with cutting-edge insights and recommendations.

How Digital Transformation is Shaping Management Consulting

1. The Role of Technology

Digital transformation is fundamentally reshaping the tools and technologies used in management consulting. Consultants now have access to a wide range of digital tools that enhance their capabilities and efficiency. For example, project management software, collaboration platforms, and communication tools enable seamless coordination and information sharing among consulting teams and clients. Furthermore, artificial intelligence (AI) and machine learning (ML) are revolutionizing data analysis, allowing consultants to derive deeper insights and develop more sophisticated models for forecasting and optimization.

2. Digital Strategy Development

One of the primary ways digital transformation is shaping management consulting is through the development of digital strategies. Consultants are increasingly tasked with helping clients formulate comprehensive digital strategies that encompass digital marketing, e-commerce, data analytics, and cybersecurity. A robust digital strategy aligns technology initiatives with business objectives, ensuring that digital investments drive tangible value. Consultants must guide clients in prioritizing digital initiatives, assessing technological readiness, and navigating the complexities of implementation.

3. Cybersecurity and Risk Management

As organizations become more digitally interconnected, cybersecurity and risk management have become critical components of management consulting. Consultants must help clients identify and mitigate cyber threats, ensuring the security and integrity of their digital assets. This involves conducting risk assessments, developing cybersecurity strategies, and implementing robust security measures. Additionally, consultants must assist clients in complying with regulatory requirements related to data privacy and protection, such as the General Data Protection Regulation (GDPR).

4. Customer Experience Optimization

Digital transformation places a strong emphasis on enhancing the customer experience. Management consultants play a pivotal role in helping clients design and implement customer-centric strategies that leverage digital technologies. This includes optimizing digital channels, such as websites and mobile apps, to provide seamless and personalized experiences. Consultants also help clients utilize customer data to gain insights into preferences, behaviors, and pain points, enabling the development of targeted marketing campaigns and loyalty programs.

5. Change Management and Culture

Successful digital transformation requires not only technological changes but also cultural and organizational shifts. Management consultants must guide clients through the change management process, addressing resistance and fostering a culture of innovation and agility. This involves developing change management plans, conducting training programs, and facilitating communication to ensure that employees are aligned with the digital vision. Consultants must also help leaders role-model digital behaviors and create an environment that encourages experimentation and learning.

6. Talent and Skills Development

The digital age demands a workforce with new skills and capabilities. Management consultants assist clients in identifying skill gaps and developing strategies for talent acquisition and development. This includes designing training programs to upskill employees in areas such as data analytics, digital marketing, and cybersecurity. Consultants also help clients build a talent pipeline by leveraging digital tools for recruitment and by fostering partnerships with educational institutions and technology providers.

7. Continuous Improvement and Innovation

Digital transformation is an ongoing journey, and management consultants must instill a mindset of continuous improvement and innovation within client organizations. This involves establishing mechanisms for monitoring progress, measuring outcomes, and iterating on strategies. Consultants should encourage clients to embrace a culture of experimentation, where failures are seen as opportunities for learning and growth. By fostering a continuous improvement mindset, consultants help clients stay ahead of the competition and adapt to evolving market conditions.

8. Sustainability and Ethical Considerations

In the digital age, sustainability and ethical considerations are increasingly important. Management consultants must guide clients in integrating sustainability into their digital strategies, ensuring that technological advancements do not come at the expense of environmental and social responsibilities. This includes advising on sustainable practices, such as reducing carbon footprints through digital solutions, and addressing ethical issues related to data privacy, AI bias, and digital inclusivity. By promoting sustainable and ethical practices, consultants help clients build a positive brand reputation and contribute to long-term societal well-being.

9. Globalization and Remote Work

Digital transformation has also facilitated globalization and the rise of remote work. Management consultants must navigate the challenges and opportunities associated with these trends. For example, consultants need to help clients manage distributed teams, optimize virtual collaboration, and address cross-cultural differences. Additionally, consultants can leverage digital tools to provide remote consulting services, expanding their reach and enabling them to serve clients globally. The ability to operate effectively in a digital and global environment is a critical skill for modern management consultants.

10. Case Studies and Success Stories

To illustrate the impact of digital transformation on management consulting, it is valuable to examine case studies and success stories. For instance, a consulting firm may have helped a traditional retail company transition to e-commerce, resulting in significant revenue growth and market expansion. Another example could be a consultant assisting a healthcare provider in implementing telehealth solutions, enhancing patient care and operational efficiency. These case studies demonstrate how digital transformation can drive tangible business outcomes and highlight the crucial role of management consultants in facilitating these transformations.

Conclusion

The fundamentals of management consulting have evolved significantly in the digital age. Consultants must now navigate a complex landscape shaped by rapid technological advancements, changing consumer behaviors, and global interconnectedness. Key principles such as understanding client needs, data-driven decision-making, agility, collaboration, and innovation remain central to effective consulting. However, the digital era demands new practices, including the development of digital strategies, cybersecurity, customer experience optimization, change management, talent development, and sustainability considerations.

By embracing these principles and practices, management consultants can guide organizations through the challenges and opportunities of digital transformation. As trusted advisors, consultants play a vital role in helping clients leverage digital technologies to drive growth, efficiency, and competitiveness. The digital age presents an exciting frontier for management consulting, where the ability to adapt, innovate, and deliver value will determine success in an ever-evolving business landscape.

Chapter 25. Leadership Development for Digital Transformation

Introduction

In the rapidly evolving digital landscape, leadership development is pivotal to navigating the complexities of digital transformation. As organizations worldwide pivot to digital-first strategies, the role of leaders becomes increasingly crucial in driving innovation, fostering a digital culture, and ensuring sustainable growth. This article delves into the essentials of building leadership skills for the digital era and explores case studies of successful leadership in digital transformation.

Building Leadership Skills for the Digital Era

In the digital era, traditional leadership skills must be augmented with new competencies to effectively manage and lead digital transformation initiatives. The following are key areas where leaders need to develop their capabilities.

1. Visionary Thinking and Strategic Foresight

Digital transformation requires leaders to possess visionary thinking and strategic foresight. Leaders must anticipate future trends, understand the potential of emerging technologies, and envision how these can be integrated into their business models. This forward-thinking approach allows organizations to stay ahead of the curve and capitalize on new opportunities.

2. Agility and Adaptability

The digital landscape is characterized by rapid change and uncertainty. Leaders must be agile and adaptable, able to respond quickly to new challenges and opportunities. This means fostering a culture of continuous learning and innovation within the organization. Leaders should encourage experimentation, embrace failure as a learning opportunity, and be willing to pivot strategies when necessary.

3. Technological Literacy

While leaders do not need to be tech experts, they must possess a fundamental understanding of digital technologies and their implications for business. This includes knowledge of data analytics, artificial intelligence, machine learning, blockchain (a decentralized, distributed ledger technology that securely records transactions across multiple computers, ensuring data integrity and transparency), and other transformative technologies. Technological literacy enables leaders to make informed decisions, understand the potential and limitations of technology, and effectively communicate with technical teams.

4. Emotional Intelligence and Change Management

Digital transformation often involves significant organizational change, which can be met with resistance. Leaders with high emotional intelligence can navigate these challenges effectively by understanding and addressing the concerns of their teams. They need to be skilled in change management, able to articulate a compelling vision, and inspire and motivate their teams to embrace the transformation journey.

5. Collaborative Leadership and Building Digital Teams

Digital transformation requires a collaborative approach, breaking down silos (fostering collaboration and communication across different departments or teams within an organization). Leaders must build and nurture high-performing digital teams, leveraging diverse skills and perspectives. This involves creating an inclusive environment where innovation can thrive and ensuring that all team members are aligned with the organization's digital vision.

Case Studies of Successful Leadership in Digital Transformation

To illustrate the impact of effective leadership on digital transformation, let's explore some case studies of organizations that have successfully navigated this journey.

1. Microsoft: Satya Nadella's Visionary Leadership

When Satya Nadella became CEO of Microsoft in 2014, the company was struggling to keep pace with the rapidly evolving tech landscape. Nadella's leadership transformed Microsoft into a cloud-first, mobile-first organization. He championed a growth mindset, encouraging employees to embrace learning and innovation. Under his leadership, Microsoft pivoted its focus to cloud computing, resulting in the success of Azure, which now competes head-to-head with Amazon Web Services (AWS). Nadella's emphasis on empathy and collaboration also reinvigorated the company culture, fostering a more inclusive and innovative environment.

2. General Electric: Embracing the Industrial Internet of Things (IIoT)

General Electric (GE) embarked on a digital transformation journey under the leadership of former CEO Jeffrey Immelt. Recognizing the potential of the Industrial Internet of Things (IIoT), Immelt steered GE towards becoming a digital industrial company. GE invested heavily in developing Predix, an industrial internet platform that enables companies to collect and analyze data from their machines to optimize performance. This transformation required a significant cultural shift and the development of new digital capabilities across the organization. Despite challenges, GE's commitment to digital innovation under Immelt's leadership positioned the company as a pioneer in the IIoT space.

3. DBS Bank: Piyush Gupta's Digital Reinvention

DBS Bank, under the leadership of CEO Piyush Gupta, undertook a comprehensive digital transformation to become the leading digital bank in Asia. Gupta's vision was to reimagine banking by leveraging technology to enhance customer experience and streamline operations. DBS invested in building digital capabilities, such as artificial intelligence, big data analytics, and cloud computing. The bank also embraced a startup culture, fostering innovation through initiatives like hackathons and innovation labs. As a result, DBS Bank has been recognized globally for its digital banking services, setting a benchmark for the industry.

Cultivating a Digital-First Culture

Successful digital transformation extends beyond technology; it involves cultivating a digital-first culture within the organization. Leaders play a critical role in shaping this culture by promoting values that support digital innovation and collaboration.

1. Encouraging Experimentation and Innovation

Leaders must create an environment where experimentation and innovation are encouraged and rewarded. This involves providing resources and support for employees to explore new ideas, test hypotheses, and learn from failures. By fostering a culture of innovation, organizations can continuously evolve and stay competitive in the digital age.

2. Fostering Continuous Learning and Development

The rapid pace of technological change necessitates continuous learning and development. Leaders should prioritize upskilling and reskilling initiatives to ensure that employees have the necessary digital competencies. This can be achieved through training programs, workshops, and partnerships with educational institutions. Additionally, leaders should lead by example, demonstrating their commitment to lifelong learning.

3. Promoting Collaboration and Cross-Functional Teams

Digital transformation often requires collaboration across different functions and departments. Leaders must break down silos and promote cross-functional teamwork. This can be achieved by establishing clear communication channels, setting collaborative goals, and recognizing the contributions of diverse teams. Collaborative leadership ensures that all parts of the organization are aligned and working towards the common goal of digital transformation.

The Role of Leadership in Overcoming Digital Transformation Challenges

Digital transformation is fraught with challenges, from technological hurdles to resistance to change. Effective leadership is crucial in overcoming these challenges and ensuring the success of digital initiatives.

1. Addressing Resistance to Change

Resistance to change is a common challenge in digital transformation. Leaders must address this by clearly communicating the vision and benefits of the transformation. This involves engaging with employees at all levels, addressing their concerns, and involving them in the transformation process. By building trust and demonstrating the value of the transformation, leaders can mitigate resistance and foster buy-in from the entire organization.

2. Ensuring Data Security and Privacy

As organizations adopt digital technologies, data security and privacy become paramount concerns. Leaders must prioritize these issues, ensuring that robust cybersecurity measures are in place to protect sensitive information. This involves investing in secure technologies, establishing data governance policies, and promoting a culture of security awareness among employees.

3. Managing Technological Integration

Integrating new technologies with existing systems can be complex and challenging. Leaders must ensure that there is a clear strategy for technological integration, including thorough planning, testing, and monitoring. This may involve collaborating with technology partners, leveraging external expertise, and ensuring that the integration aligns with the organization's overall digital strategy.

Conclusion: The Path Forward

Leadership development for digital transformation is not a one-time effort but an ongoing journey. As the digital landscape continues to evolve, leaders must remain agile, continuously update their skills, and foster a culture of innovation and collaboration within their organizations. By embracing visionary thinking, technological literacy, emotional intelligence, and collaborative leadership, leaders can successfully navigate the complexities of digital transformation and drive their organizations towards sustainable growth and success.

In conclusion, the digital era demands a new breed of leaders who are not only equipped with traditional leadership skills but also possess the agility, foresight, and technological savvy to lead their organizations through the challenges and opportunities of digital transformation. By learning from successful case studies and cultivating a digital-first culture, organizations can develop the leadership capabilities needed to thrive in the digital age.

Other Books by the Author

- Life in Multinational Companies
- Entrepreneurship in the Digital Landscape
- A Guide to SEO Executive Skills
- Challenges in IT and Digital Marketing
- Life and Challenges of IT Professionals
- Women Entrepreneurs in the Modern World
- Artificial Intelligence and Its Transformative Impact on Society
- Comprehensive Guide for IT Job Applicants: Key Questions and Answers

"A Comprehensive Guide to Digital Marketing" is an all-encompassing resource that delves into the core aspects and advanced techniques of digital marketing. This book covers essential topics such as SEO, SEM, content marketing, and social media strategies, ensuring readers grasp both foundational concepts and cutting-edge practices. Each chapter, from leveraging AI in SEO to effective blogging and influencer marketing, is designed to equip professionals with practical tools and insights. Detailed guides on platforms like SEMrush and Google Analytics, coupled with chapters on mobile marketing, video content creation, and e-commerce strategies, make this book an invaluable asset for anyone looking to excel in the digital marketing landscape.

ABOUT THE AUTHOR

Mr. C. P. Kumar is a retired Scientist 'G' from National Institute of Hydrology, Roorkee, Uttarakhand, India. He is also a Reiki Healer and Chakra Balancing practitioner (with pendulum dowsing) and offers Emotional Freedom Technique (EFT) to help individuals with emotional issues. Mr. Kumar has authored many books on technical, spiritual, and social topics.

For further details, you may visit his webpage
https://www.angelfire.com/nh/cpkumar/virgo.html

www.ingramcontent.com/pod-product-compliance
Lightning Source LLC
Chambersburg PA
CBHW071919210526
45479CB00002B/485